Tragic Vision
and Divine
Compassion

"A voice is heard in Ramah,
   lamentation and bitter weeping.
Rachel is weeping for her children;
   she refuses to be comforted for her children,
   because they are not."

Thus says the LORD:
"Keep your voice from weeping,
   and your eyes from tears;
for your work shall be rewarded, says the LORD,
   and they shall come back from the land of the enemy.
There is hope for your future, says the LORD."

Jeremiah 31:15–17

Contents

Preface

Those twin faces of evil—sin and suffering—have assaulted us in this century with terrible intensity. The world witnessed something of an apotheosis of evil when technology, fascism, and antisemitism combined to orchestrate the murder of some six million Jews at the hands of the Nazis. While the cruelty of this evil is unmatched, the villainy of Stalin, Pol Pot, and paramilitary death squads around the globe makes the statistics themselves rather modest by comparison. War ravages every continent, while hunger murders countless millions with less fanfare but no less savagery. Bombs that could destroy all life on the planet are suspended over our heads by the slimmest of threads.

And yet we remain out of tune with our times. The sweetness of insanity is our truest consolation. Surely it is insanity that in the face of massive evil and imminent destruction, many Americans' primary preoccupation is to be entertained—and not really entertained, merely distracted. The passionate need to escape—through drugs, alcohol, relentless work, or the banalities of the media—has become a national pathology.

I feel no smug disgust at other people's insanity. I share it. Human history has been so badly stained by suffering that it cannot be endured. It has become literally meaningless. Attempts to bring order to this chaos through secular myths of progress, the worship of technology, and dreams of personal success are mocked by the destruction all around us. Religion used to be a panacea; Christians could at least be confident that evil came about through sin and was therefore just punishment. There would be rest and vindication in heaven. But these consolations pale and shiver when exposed to the sight of radical suffering. Neither secular nor religious promises are robust enough to survive the evil and suffering our century has unleashed.

I have found the history I live in intolerable and the solutions of classical Christian theodicy unhelpful. Augustine watched as the barbarians of the north spread destruction like a virus through what was to him the entire known world and the apex of civilization. But his theory of predestination seems as morally bankrupt as the violence that surrounded him. Thomas Aquinas lived in more placid times, but surely even he should have known something about the harshness of medieval life. Was Calvin too innocent or too cruel to imagine the possibility of unjust and destructive suffering? Why do these men, so brilliant in other ways, have so little wisdom to offer those who suffer?

Armed with neither the learning nor the intelligence of the classical theologians, I have entered into the murky, hopeless regions of theodicy. I break with this theological tradition that I love in three ways. First, I place suffering rather than sin at the center of the problem of evil. I do this not because I do not think sin is a problem but because I think suffering is a more serious anomaly for Christian faith. I am particularly concerned about what I call "radical suffering": suffering that has the power to dehumanize and degrade human beings (for example, child abuse or death camps) and that cannot be traced to punishment or desert.

Second, the conceptual environment of my reflections is one governed by tragedy rather than by the Fall. Christian theology has tended to be strenuously antitragic. At the beginning of history is a Fall that justifies suffering by interpreting it as a consequence of sin. At the end of history is the eschatological return to harmony, the cosmic overcoming of evil, and the redemption of the elect. The drama of salvation is firmly contained within a moral vision while anticipating a comic outcome. It is the neatness of this vision that disturbs me. It quells outrage over suffering by *explaining* it and, worse, by justifying it. I find myself in the company of Ivan Karamazov, who refuses to be comforted by any theodicy—purgation, punishment, vindication, harmony, retribution. None of these can make it all right that children are tortured by their parents or their governments. At best these explanations make it easier not to mind other people's suffering so much. Moralism moves too quickly to palliatives that obscure the cruelty of evil.

I am drawn to tragedy because it retains the sharp edge of anger at the unfairness and destructiveness of suffering. I explore a tragic vision in order to find categories for evil that do not justify or explain suffering. Tragedy is not gnosticism; it is rooted in a deep sense of the value of creation. Tragedy is driven by a desire for justice, but it does not find this desire satisfied in history. Nor does tragedy consider speculations about a Fall or eschatological harmony adequate substitutes for historical justice and compassion.

Third, I repudiate the assumption that the power to dominate is an appropriate model for divine power. The metaphors of judge and king, the concept of omnipotence, do little to illuminate the radical alterity (otherness) and goodness of divine perfection. I have attempted to think through the logic of a different *kind* of power, power that is modeled on a phenomenology of love rather than domination. I use compassion, as a form of love, to symbolize the distinctiveness of redemptive power.

Although I am by training and disposition very much a neophyte in methodological issues, a few remarks on my method may help the reader make some sense out of my argument. Most generally, my method is phenomenological-descriptive. I have tried to describe my subject matter in such a way as to evoke a spark of recognition in the reader. I have tried to anchor my reflections as firmly as possible in concrete experience and toward this end have scattered illustrations—from history, literature, or the Bible—throughout the text.

I tend not to appeal to authorities—biblical, theological, or philosophical—although I rely very heavily on all three of these traditions. As a Protestant and feminist, I am skeptical of all authorities. I have tried to be ruthless in weeding out quotations and examinations of other people's arguments—keeping my eye on the ball, as it were, and avoiding scholarly digressions. My dialogues with other thinkers go on mostly behind closed doors. The attentive reader will find echoes of these discussions, though, sprinkled throughout the argument. I am indebted to too many thinkers to list them, but those who stalk through this text with particular frequency include Emmanuel Levinas, Paul Ricoeur, Paul Tillich, Emil Fackenheim, Sharon Welch, Thomas Aquinas, Rebecca Chopp, Rosemary Radford Ruether, John Calvin, and Julian of Norwich. I am ashamed to admit it, but Plato has also left certain traces.

I have what still seems even to me the shocking temerity to bring up God in the following discussion. In attempting the absurd task of relating transcendent power to historical evil, I have been most dependent on the dialectic between affirmative and negative theology inaugurated by Pseudo-Dionysius the Areopagite. Negation qualifies every symbol, statement, or experience concerning divine being. No method or authority assuages the radical and unsurpassable alterity of God. But the logic of causality provides a basis for affirmative theology. If one begins with the assumption that finitude is dependent upon the infinite (a theological assumption that can be neither proven nor abandoned by a person of faith), affirmations emerge that symbolize the power of divine causality.

One cannot make assertions about God's own being, but it is possible to describe the *effects* of God. Friedrich Schleiermacher provides a more recent example of this method. Schleiermacher found the decisive clue to theology in the experience of redemption. For him, redemption refers to the mediation of God-consciousness to people and to history. He reasoned that since God is the cause of redemption, the most proper designation for God is love.

I have constructed a response to the problem of suffering and evil on the basis of a phenomenology of divine love. The status of my theological claims is, at best, symbolic. As Tillich argues, a symbol opens up a region or level of reality, but it is not identical to that reality. I am unwilling to reduce theology to descriptions of cultural, sociological, or psychological prejudices. Nor am I content to appeal to authorities, as if anything in history could magically escape limitation and corruption by culture, society, and psychology. Following Schleiermacher, I find the essential clue to theological claims in the experience of redemption: more specifically, in examples of the resistance to evil within history. Following Pseudo-Dionysius, I know that all my claims, arguments, and symbols are grossly inadequate to their subject matter and in fact cannot touch the reality of God.

A project such as this one is possible only because there are people around to support it in various ways. I am grateful to Vanderbilt University and to Emory University, both of which provided me with grant money at different stages of the project. Theologian or not, I am not indifferent to the usefulness of cold hard cash.

I have been very moved by the support and encouragement I have received from my colleagues at Emory, who have already had certain aspects of the argument inflicted on them. I am especially grateful for the encouragement I received from Vernon Robbins and David Blumenthal. Lisseth Rojas and Lyn Schechtel have provided me with a good deal of technical and personal support, for which I thank them.

Bettye Ford at Vanderbilt's Department of Religion has been a guardian angel to me for many years, for which I feel the profoundest appreciation.

Betty Deberg, Ellen Armour, and Jody Combs are friends and colleagues who have provided me with comfort, advice, and much-needed solace. More to the point, they have shared with me their computer expertise. Without the first, I would just be more bad-tempered; but without the second, I would still be waiting tables. (The pen may have been good enough for St. Anselm, but it is no longer a powerful enough tool with which to do theology.) For both kinds of help, I am speechless with gratitude.

Davis Perkins at Westminster/John Knox Press has provided me with the advantage of a truly kind and insightful editor. His advice with regard to style and substance was always right on the money. It has been a pleasure and an honor to work with him.

The argument as it appears now in its final form has been through a number of stages and incarnations. I am deeply grateful for the careful reading, time, patience, and good advice I received from Sallie McFague and Peter Hodgson. It is because of their help that I got as far with the argument as I did, and I owe them a debt that will be difficult to repay. I am also grateful to Walter Harrelson, John Compton, and Gene TeSelle, who were generous with their time and their advice in reading the original manuscript.

In a different sense, it is to my parents, each in their own way, that I am particularly indebted. They have taught me my most profound lessons in the meaning and power of compassion. With respect to this piece of writing, the encouragement and support of my father has meant more to me than words can say.

It is customary at this point to thank one's wife: (a) for long-suffering patience and (b) for typing several thousand pages' worth of manuscript. Hating to disavow such a venerable tradition, I give my thanks and appreciation to my husband, Clifford Grabhorn, for providing me with a computer and for using his not insignificant cabinetmaking skills to build two very beautiful worktables for me.

Perhaps most of all, I acknowledge with awe and gratitude the constellation of people, good luck, and opportunities that have made it possible for me to do the work I like most.

PART ONE

Tragedy, Suffering,
and the Problem of Evil

1

Tragic Vision

O Hades, all receiving, whom no sacrifice can appease!
Hast thou no mercy for me?

Sophocles, *Antigone*

Evil as manifest in cruelty, injustice, and suffering is not simply "tragic," particularly if tragedy evokes a sense of pathetic inevitability. Guilt and suffering cannot be understood simply as subjection to an inexplicable, irrational fate. Yet there is an element of the irrational in evil that evades clear concepts and orderly judgments. No conceptual scheme can thoroughly expel the bewilderment suffering evokes. The phenomenon of human suffering continues to bleed through the explanations that attempt to account for it.

Confidence in cosmic justice cannot completely obscure the rapacity of suffering as it devours the innocent and the helpless. Hopes in future vindication do not make hunger, racism, war, and oppression theologically irrelevant. It would be consoling to believe that suffering is a consequence of wrongdoing. But the correlation between suffering and punishment is exploded by genocide in Germany and Cambodia, by the torture of prisoners of conscience, by battered women and abused children—by the "human tears with which our earth is soaked from crust to core."[1]

The cruelty of human suffering defies attempts to incorporate it into any order of justice. Instead of the just world we might envision, we seem to live in a tragic one. At least, a study of tragedy may enable theology to look at the problem of evil in a new light and to take suffering more seriously.

A deep passion for justice characterizes many of the biblical writings. This passion is seen both in the attempts to interpret Israel's suffering as just punishment and in the failure of these attempts. The Deuteronomistic historian tried desperately to contain the story of Israel's rise and fall within an ethical vision of reality. From Judges to Second Kings, the refrain is repeated: "and the people of Israel did what was evil in the sight of the Lord." The catastrophes of war, defeat, and exile are strained through ethical categories: the good are blessed and the evil punished. The defeat and destruction of Israel might be bearable if they could be made to express the justice, however painful, of a righteous God. Punishment for evildoing is terrible, but it reveals the ultimate goodness and justice of the cosmic order.

Yet, something about the destruction of Jerusalem and its people seeped through the ethical vision of the Deuteronomistic historian. A tragic interpretation of suffering competes with an ethical one. A psalmist sees Israel sold "like sheep for slaughter" and can find no reason in it:

> All this has come upon us,
>   though we have not forgotten thee,
>   or been false to thy covenant.
> Our heart has not turned back,
>   nor have our steps departed from thy way,
> that thou shouldst have broken us in the place of jackals,
>   and covered us with deep darkness.
>
> Psalm 44:17–19

The biblical writers craved justice, sometimes preferring guilt and punishment to the emptiness of chaos and absurdity. But history did little to satisfy this longing. Israel was swallowed by Babylon, the bloodthirsty world power. It was later to know persecution at the hands of the Greeks and terror and slavery at the hands of the Romans. The law of history affords victory to the strong, however cruel.

The sufferings of Israel are a microcosm of the rest of history. Humanity thirsts for justice, but we live in a world where little girls are raped and beaten by their fathers and where war ravages the most helpless and wretched of the earth's children. The hollow face of hunger does not seem to pursue only those who "deserve" to starve.

Christianity has long struggled with the need to understand the existence of evil in a world that faith insists is ordered by a gracious and powerful God. Its reflections on evil tended to be governed by the problematic of sin. The corruption of creation through human guilt, together with the atonement and forgiveness that healed creation, provided the paradigm through which evil and redemption were conceived. In this drama dominated by the Fall, suffering was relatively insignificant. Four kinds of theodicy emerged, which individually or in combination seemed to account for the brutalities of history. Sin and suffering were variously accounted for as punishment for sin, as elements of a larger aesthetic harmony, as purgation or pedagogy, or as presaging eschatological correction.

But there is a kind of suffering that destroys the power of these theodicies to spirit away the problem of evil. I am calling this phenomenon "radical suffering." The distinguishing features of radical suffering are that it is destructive of the human spirit and that it cannot be understood as something deserved. Consider the testimony of a Chilean torture victim:

> At one point, I realized that my daughter was in front of me. I even managed to touch her: I felt her hands. "Mummy, say something, anything to make this stop," she was saying. I tried to embrace her but they prevented me. They separated us violently. They took her to an adjacent room and there, there I listened in horror as they began to torture her with electricity! When I heard her moans, her terrible screams, I couldn't take it any more. I thought I would go mad, that my head and my entire body were going to explode.[2]

The obscenity of such an event annihilates the possibility of soothing ourselves with theories that justify the ways of God in an evil world. In the wake of such wanton cruelty, defenses of a divine order of justice become bitter mockeries.

Appeals to punishment and original sin to justify the torture of a mother and her child betray the ethical sensibilities that may have originally generated a penal theodicy. Attempts to include such extreme and unfair suffering within a paradigm of guilt and punishment offers, in Kant's words, "an apology in which the defense is worse than the charge . . . and may certainly be left to the detestation of everyone who has the least spark of morality."[3]

Thomas Aquinas argues that evil does not significantly undermine the goodness of creation. Particular creatures may suffer, but the diminishment of particular creatures is necessary to the good of the whole. "For if all evil were prevented much good would be absent from the universe."[4] Creation is good because the whole is good. This aesthetic metaphysics turns our eyes to the beauty of the cosmos by rendering particular sufferings invisible. But justice cannot tolerate a cosmic harmony whose edifice is maintained on the unavenged tears of tormented children.

It might be argued that suffering is good for people: it makes them stronger, more sensitive, more mature. It is true that suffering sometimes has this effect. But radical suffering destroys its victims, it does not make them stronger. Assuming that she survives, is it likely that the Chilean child will be a better person for having electric shocks applied to her fingers and toes? Such suffering is of another order than that which might be pedagogical.

Eschatology can console those who find no refuge in history. It can attest to a hope that evil is not the last word. But it is in history that we live, struggle, think, act, and suffer. Without denying the legitimacy of eschatological hopes, theology must seek a historical response to evil. Otherwise, consolation and hope may degenerate into excuses for remaining passive or indifferent in the face of radical suffering and injustice.

Theodicy cannot take the sting out of evil: the surd of destructive suffering remains. The longing for justice, for an ethical order, is not satisfied by historical experience. Neither is it satisfied by theories that attempt to obscure the horror of evil or justify the existence of suffering. In the face of radical suffering, traditional theodicies are unable to exorcise the demons that whisper that life is futile, suffering meaningless, and the cosmos an empty and evil void.

Tragedy enters into the hiatus between the longing for justice and the reality of suffering. Unlike traditional theodicies, tragedy does not attempt to penetrate the opacity of evil by providing justifications of suffering. It recognizes that certain kinds of suffering are irredeemably unjust. It sees justice languishing in history, where the innocent are destroyed while their murderers are honored and feted. The mothers of the "disappeared" in El Salvador are tortured and condemned as "terrorists," while their tormentors are celebrated in Washington. Jesus writhes on the cross; Herod and Pilate become friends.

A tragic sense of life burns with a desire for justice, but, unlike theodicy, burns even more with anger and pity at suffering. In tragic vision, unassuaged indignation and compassionate resistance replace theodicy's cool justifications of evil.

Historical Background

Job, Lamentations, the story of Saul, and certain psalms represent traces of a tragic sensibility in the Bible. But tragedy as a distinct literary genre begins with the Athenian playwrights, Aeschylus, Sophocles, and Euripides. Although the ancient tragedians gave profound expression to tragedy, sensitivity to tragic dimensions of existence reaches far beyond this literary genre. Unamuno describes tragedy as a distinct "sense of life."[5] Max Scheler, Karl Jaspers, and Nicolas Berdyaev interpret tragedy as central to ethical and religious experience.[6] While there is no complete agreement on what constitutes tragedy, certain themes emerge with some regularity: attentiveness to suffering, freedom and responsibility, a world order that distorts this freedom, and resistance to tragic suffering. These elements will be examined in turn.

Suffering

W. Lee Humphreys argues that "at the heart of tragic vision lies human suffering, suffering triggered in important ways by the action of the hero, yet suffering that is necessary at the very core of the human situation in the world. In the face of this necessary suffering the hero does not remain passive."[7] Humphreys's description hits several of the key elements of tragedy: action, external necessity, and resistance. But it is suffering itself that holds these elements together. Philosophers, theologians, playwrights, and novelists are in unanimous agreement that whatever else is entailed in tragedy, suffering lies at its very heart. This concern with suffering distinguishes tragedy from most Christian theology, which identifies guilt as the primary clue to the human condition.

While suffering is the essential subject matter of tragedy,

suffering may be pathetic, cruel, or miserable without being tragic. Tragic suffering is distinguished by its destructive power and its irreducibility to fault. The poignancy of tragic suffering is especially pronounced when the hero is very good but is destroyed by something beyond his or her control. The destruction of a passionately good person makes the unfairness of tragic suffering nearly intolerable. There is nothing to appeal to which would make this suffering meaningful. It is antithetical to even the crudest notions of justice since it cannot be traced to punishment. It is not pedagogical since it cannot strengthen or purify the person. Tragic heroes and heroines are usually destroyed in the course of the story. Antigone is zealous in her piety and loyalty but ends by hanging herself. Prometheus teaches and protects human beings out of pity but is hurled into the abyss by Zeus. The suffering is raw, unmediated by justice or utility; it witnesses to the power of absurdity or malice or sheer force to bring down what is noble and good.

Freedom and Responsibility

As Humphreys's definition of tragedy indicates, tragic suffering requires some action on the part of the hero. Tragedy does not portray human beings as passive puppets; people act and are responsible for the consequences of their actions. But neither does tragedy imagine that human action is unconstrained. Freedom is confined within a preexisting situation and is hedged by ignorance and conflict. Tragedy requires of its hero action within a situation where all action leads to disaster.

It is the genius of tragedy to recognize the complexity of responsibility. The Fates do not absolve the tragic hero from accountability, but neither is suffering resolved into penalty for negligent or corrupt freedom. Without real choice there may be pathos in suffering but not tragedy. Without a tragically structured environment, there is the justice of retribution but, again, not tragedy.

In Greek tragedy, *hubris* (zeal, passion, excess, wantonness) and *hamartia* (error, ignorance) conspire with the Fates to defraud the hero of control over a situation. Tragedy is heightened where there is action, responsibility, defeat, but little or no real sense of guilt. The action that condemns the hero is a guiltless action. Oedipus's compulsive search for the truth evinces a moral zeal that has the ironic consequence of destroying him. His integrity is condemned beforehand by his ignorance of his true situation. His ruin cannot be traced to any wickedness or selfishness on his part. According to the information at his disposal, he was a brave, intelligent Greek citizen with the good fortune of winning a kingdom and a lovely wife. Oedipus was not in a position to know he was committing patricide and incest. Although he was deceived about his real situation, ignorance did not prevent the inner dynamic of his actions from bearing down on him. Oedipus's actions brought about his downfall, but not in the sense that punishment follows crime. Freedom is betrayed, but responsibility remains intact.

> Actions count, and choices are made in confrontation with genuine alternatives. In this we are responsible for our deeds and reap what we sow. Yet this freedom to decide and act is exercised on a larger stage on which factors and forces beyond our control, and often even beyond our understanding, govern our lives. Our freedom is neither absolute nor overall. . . . The stage on which freedom is exercised is in many essentials defined for us, and it is the nature of that larger arena that is of basic concern in the tragic vision.[8]

Tragedy recognizes something in the world order recalcitrant to human freedom and well-being, which qualifies and even corrupts obligation. But tragedy resists the temptation to elevate this enigmatic necessity to a strict determinism or predestination that would erode responsibility. The dialectic between freedom and fate remains ambiguous. Human beings are not absolved from responsibility, but actions are performed in an environment that is not morally neutral; it is already tainted, disguised, even malevolent.

An Element of the World Order

Justice can hardly tolerate an event in which a particularly virtuous person is defeated by his or her own moral passion, but tragedy goes further. It is not an accident that misery and failure come to those who least deserve them. Tragic suffering is not a consequence of a Fall or a cathartic exception that reinstates the reign of justice. Something in the constitution of the world makes an ethical passion for piety, justice, truth, or compassion self-destructive. The world order itself is implicated as the origin of tragic suffering.

The real subject matter of tragedy is not an individual who errs or sins and so brings catastrophe on herself. Particular cases of tragic suffering are meant to *exemplify* a world order in which intolerable and unjustifiable suffering is inevitable. "The remote subject of the tragic is always the world itself, the world taken as a whole which makes such things possible."⁹ The catastrophes that befall tragic heroes illuminate the *way things really are.*

Tragedy describes suffering that is caused, at least in part, by some aspect of reality over which the hero has no control. The environment of tragedy is usually either an external, non-human power (such as the Fates or Zeus) or a set of intrinsically conflicting values. In the first case, tragic suffering comes about because the hero's moral passion is in conflict with ultimate powers of the cosmos. The nymphs sing to Prometheus, who is bound to a rock:

> None so hard of heart can be, joys to see thy misery;
> None but watches sorrowful, none save Zeus the all-powerful.¹⁰

Prometheus is punished for his kindness to the human race. The compassion that he incarnates in his actions is in fundamental conflict with the order of the cosmos represented by the omnipotent Zeus. In a cosmos ordered by principles of sheer power, compassion is dangerous and self-destructive.

In the second kind of tragedy, the conflict among values is presented as an element of the world order. Tragedy is not traced to a malevolent cosmic force but rather to the essential irreconcilability of equally important obligations. Antigone is passionate in her insistence that she must honor her duties to the gods and to her family by burying her renegade brother. Her piety, unfortunately, cannot coexist with loyalty to the authority of the government. She cannot fulfill her obligations to the gods and her family and also obey Creon's prohibition against burying traitors. She exemplifies the passion for justice that is condemned by an environment that *requires* a betrayal of one fundamental value in order to pursue another.¹¹

Tragedy portrays a world in which the virtuous are the most vulnerable to suffering and destruction. The passion for good puts the hero in conflict either with a malevolent cosmos or with some other good. This by itself challenges ethical descriptions of the world order in which the righteous person prospers and the wicked perish. Tragedy not only introduces the anomaly of unjust suffering into the moral order of the cosmos, it questions whether such a moral order exists.

Resistance

Tragedy is ethical, however, rather than nihilistic. The tragedies of ancient Greece are unrelenting in their depiction of the downfall of the noble and virtuous, but they are not cynical. Tragic heroes are not resigned or stoic or glib: they are defiant. The tenacity of Prometheus or Antigone in the face of torment and death discloses a kernel of integrity that remains untarnished. The ethical vitality of the tragic hero attests to a moral order that is vindicated by their actions, even though they are destroyed in the process.

In tragedy, the power of evil to destroy what is good is present in the very structure of the cosmos. But then another layer of the world order is peeled back. One is permitted to glimpse something beyond the apparent finality of evil. The victory of the malignant power suddenly rings hollow. An ethical order reappears to stand in judgment on that which would defeat what is good. As Prometheus is hurled into the black void, he appeals to the goddess of justice:

> Oh, holy mother mine, oh light of heaven,
> That sheddest radiance on all things that are,
> Thou, thou canst see the injustice of my fate.[12]

Even in defeat, a vision of justice remains to vindicate the tragic hero. The defiance of the hero enacts and recovers human dignity even in the teeth of destruction. If suffering and destruction cannot be overcome, they can be resisted. It is in the resistance itself, in this refusal to give up the passion for justice, that tragedy is transcended. "Tragic knowledge always contains the final release from tragedy, not through doctrine and revelation, but through the vision of order, justice, love of one's fellow man; through trust; through an open mind and the acceptance of the questions as such, unanswered."[13]

The resilience of tragedy's passion for justice is epitomized in Aeschylus's *Prometheus Bound*. The conflict between a savage cosmic order and the order of justice is personified in the contest between Zeus and Prometheus. Omnipotent Zeus is driven only by lascivious self-interest. His power is consummated in egotistical cravings and violence. He personifies a cosmos or history in which "justice" means nothing but the rapaciousness of sheer power.

In contrast, Prometheus is the embodiment of compassion. He teaches human beings medicine, art, and agriculture out of pity for their ignorance and helplessness. The reward for this service is to be impaled on a rock by Zeus's minions, Force and Might. Human beings present no threat to Zeus, but he is goaded by Prometheus's gratuitous kindness. The play concludes with Prometheus being hurled into Tartarus. It would appear that pity is finally defeated by Force and that the order epitomized by Zeus's cruelty is the final word.

Prometheus enjoys the gift of foresight. He knows that he will eventually be released from his bondage. He also knows that Zeus, the ravager of mortal women, will take Thetis as a wife, and the child of that match will be his murderer. Prometheus, alone among gods and mortals, can prevent the downfall of Zeus by revealing to him that it is Thetis who is the sign of his destruction. But Zeus's cruelty has made Prometheus his unending foe. Prometheus gladly shares his knowledge with another of Zeus's victims, Io, to relieve her suffering. But none of Zeus's tortures can prevail upon him to help Zeus escape his fate. The brutality of power wins, but only by ensuring its own downfall. There will be another day.

The suffering of the tragic hero evokes pity; it is painful to watch a good person suffer. This suffering uncovers a world order that is hostile to what is good or virtuous. The defeat of the tragic hero suggests that the cosmos is meaningless and violent. This is the horror of tragedy. Tragedy penetrates to the dark heart of human experience where it is haunted by destruction at the hands of a chaotic, savage cosmos. But tragedy does not rest there. The experience of unfairness and defeat is real, but it is not absolute. Something remains untainted, even impervious to the power of Zeus or the persistent Fates. Some vision of justice or a hope for vindication survives. Notwithstanding the might of Zeus or the conflict of values, some good persists that makes defiance of tragedy meaningful.

When the tragic becomes absolute, it is no longer tragic but nihilistic. The Greek tragedies presuppose a moral order that is absent in Beckett or Ionesco. The suffering of Antigone or Prometheus is horrible, but it is not absurd. Tragedy presses upon us a dark vision of reality, but it is in turn transcended by the apprehension of ultimate goodness. Its appeal to justice and its evocation of compassion are traces of an ethical order that is frustrated but not destroyed by unjust suffering. Still, if a vision of justice finally transcends the tragic, it is not by denying its existence. Tragedy remains a perennial qualification of existence. It is redeemed but not abolished. "As *agent provocateur,* it is a stone in the path. . . . Those humans who will endure for more than a season . . . will be those who have been able to take up the stone that is the tragic vision . . . and set it as the cornerstone for their structure."[14]

Features of the Tragic Vision

Tragic vision is deeply shaped by the biblical passion for justice and by Greek tragedy's preoccupation with suffering. It is driven by a deep sense of justice but does not devolve justice into patterns of reward and punishment. Neither Greek tragedy nor the biblical writings are limited by a penal understanding of justice. The more characteristic ethical problem both literatures address is the *injustice* of certain events and sufferings rather than the *justice* of punishing sinners. Justice is restored not so much when Nebuchadnezzar or Zeus is punished, but when Israel or Prometheus is vindicated and relieved of persecution.

Radical suffering confronts theology with a problem that cannot be addressed within the context of the myth of the Fall. A theology governed by the thematics of guilt does not have the tools to recognize or respond to the existence of unjust and destructive suffering. As an alternative to this paradigm, tragic vision locates the possibility of suffering in the conditions of existence and in the fragility of human freedom. The very structures that make human existence possible make us subject to the destructive power of suffering. Since guilt is not the primary problem, atonement and forgiveness cannot help transcend tragedy. Tragic suffering cannot be atoned for; it must be defied. Compassion is that power which survives to resist tragic suffering.

Suffering

The suffering that is of particular concern for tragedy is that which has the effect of destroying its victims and which cannot be understood as being deserved. Sickness, separation from loved ones, and death cause suffering and should evoke compassion and help from most moderately decent persons. But they do not necessarily suggest a tragic or broken world order.

When innocent or good people are destroyed by suffering, a new problem emerges that cannot be easily contained within a moral order. Ivan Karamazov uses the example of child abuse as an example of an evil so intense, so vile that it destroys the possibility even of future harmony. A created order that permits the torment of innocent children is, for Ivan, so fundamentally corrupt that nothing can ever heal it. A moral person must be in rebellion against any deity who would create such a world.

> There's [a story] about a little five-year-old girl, hated by her parents, who are described as "most respectable and socially prominent people, cultured and well-educated." . . . And so these refined parents subjected their five-year-old girl to all kinds of torture. They beat her, kicked her, flogged her, for no reason that they themselves knew of. The child's whole body was covered with bruises. Eventually they devised a new refinement . . . they forced her to eat excrement, smearing it all over her face. And it was her mother who did it! And then that woman would lock her little daughter up in the outhouse until morning and she did so even on the coldest nights, when it was freezing. Imagine the little creature, unable even to understand what is happening to her, beating her sore little chest with her tiny fist, weeping hot, unresentful tears, and begging "gentle Jesus" to help her, and all this happening in that icy, dark, stinking place![15]

The example of child abuse may seem insignificant beside the atrocities of genocide in Cambodia or mass murder in Central America. Domestic violence is commonplace, hardly even a crime. That is why it serves as an illustration of tragic suffering: it is suffering that is directed against the weak and helpless, that can cripple the very humanity of its victims, and that is *ordinary*. Child abuse exemplifies the way in which destructive suffering can invade everyday existence. In Ivan's example, the child is not abused by criminals but by decent and respected people. Theologies of liberation have begun to sensitize us to the massive scale of suffering caused by institutional oppression. Another face of evil is what Hannah Arendt calls its banality. Evil is perpetrated by ordinary citizens and has become so commonplace that it is virtually invisible. Intense, degrading, destructive suffering is not the dramatic, horrible exception: it is the rule.

The tragic vision peers into the face of suffering and is forever marked by what it sees. It is impossible to look into the faces of the victims of suffering—in Nazi death camps; in America's urban ghettos; in torture chambers in South Africa, Chile, or Syria; in starving Latin American communities; or in middle-class homes where women and children are beaten or raped by the "head of the household"—and not feel the concrete horror and despair of human pain. No rationalization can tame this outrage or replace the hideous visage of suffering with a more palatable mask.

Post-Holocaust Jewish and Christian theologies cannot retain their authenticity without immersing themselves in the innocent suffering of the world.[16] A tragic vision is a way of preserving the undisguised horror of human suffering as an essential component of theological reflection.

> Due to the sheer numbers of victims, the increased awareness of their plights, and the widespread belief that it could be otherwise, these events erupt within history with shattering intensity. . . . Suffering and its quest for freedom is the fundamental reality of human experience as well as the location of God, Christ, and the church of history.[17]

Finitude

Tragedy places evil within a context that is more inclusive than human fault. This is not to say that sin, guilt, cruelty, and indifference have no role in evil. But all human action occurs in an environment that is not entirely shaped by human decision or desire. Tragic vision is theistic and repudiates the metaphors of a savage god or malevolent cosmos. But finitude itself seems to be tragically structured: the conditions of finite existence include conflict and fragility. This tragic structure is not evil, but it makes suffering both possible and inevitable prior to any human action. The following analysis identifies certain features of existence as simultaneously conditioning the possibility of human life and occasioning its destruction. The speculative question as to whether or not conflict, embodiment, mortality, and history are strictly speaking *necessary* to the possibility of human existence is put aside in favor of the more descriptive claim that, necessary or not, these are features of life as we know it.

Tragic vision is not gnostic; it shares with classical Christian theology a belief that creation is good. "All that is, is good," as Augustine affirms. Multiplicity and variety enrich and perfect creation.[18] Because individual creatures exist in social and ecological relationships with each other, creation is better than it would be if each entity were an isolated monad. Creation is good, creatures are good, and their mutual relationships are good.

However, relationships can be conflicted and sometimes are necessarily so, as in the relationship between predator and prey. The multiplicity of religions, cultures, and nations gives depth to human life, but this plurality inevitably (if not necessarily) degenerates into competition, misunderstanding, and conflict. Diversity becomes the occasion for suspicion and violence.

Values, too, can be essentially incommensurate and conflicting. For instance, pursuit of artistic or scientific excellence may leave little time to understand or react to social and political problems. But this benign neglect leaves the political and economic powers unfettered in their pursuit of unjust policies. Nicolas Berdyaev describes the moral life as fundamentally tragic because equally compelling values must necessarily come into conflict.

> A moral value in the narrow sense of the word comes into conflict with a cognitive or aesthetic value, a personal value with a superpersonal one. . . . A man is bound to be cruel because he is confronted with the necessity of sacrificing one value for the sake of another—for instance, of sacrificing his family for the sake of his country or of the struggle for social justice.[19]

Conflict is both a constituent feature of existence and a corruption of variety and relationship. Conflict transforms the good of religious diversity into religious persecution and war. It transforms the good of artistic genius into culpable indifference to social injustice. Conflict at once makes human life possible and suffering inevitable.

In addition to conflict, finitude is subject to decay, frustration, hurt, and death. Embodiment in a natural, material world may be the most basic feature of human life, but it subjects human beings to an assortment of dangers and sufferings.

An exploding star is very beautiful as it passes out of existence, but when mortality is accompanied by nerve endings and self-consciousness, then physical pain, grief, fear, and anxiety will augment injury and sickness with deeper kinds of sufferings. Since human beings are always social and cultural, frailty will extend itself to include culturally determined meanings and threats. A retarded or handicapped person may be excluded from society to an extent not warranted by the physical limitation itself. Bodies equipped to experience pain and pleasure can also be tortured, raped, or imprisoned. Embodiment makes it possible to experience all sorts of pleasures; mortality limits suffering with the final promise of death. But embodiment and mortality are also the causes of the most intense pain and deepest sense of foreboding.

Certain goods are possible only in conjunction with certain evils. Process theologians note the metaphysical conflict between overcoming "unnecessary triviality" and preserving harmony.[20] The intensity of enjoyment that comes from risk gives a greater perfection to creation than a flatter, if safer, world would allow. But this metaphysical conflict means that every good conceals a shadow side. Love must make a tacit agreement to lose what it most delights in. The happiness of being in love is shrouded at one end with loss and grief. Likewise, historical existence enables human beings to deepen their understanding of the world through science, art, politics, religion, and so on. But historical institutions also bear the prejudices, hatreds, and idolatries of a people through time, giving them ever increasing authority and intractable power. Christianity's depth and richness are possible because it has endured over a long period of time, addressing itself to a variety of situations, experiences, philosophies, and cultures. But the institutional authority of Christianity is also what gives continuity to its misogyny and patriarchy.

The conditions of finite existence are tragically structured. Multiplicity, embodiment, mortality, historicity make human existence possible—but each of these structures makes certain kinds of suffering inevitable.

Human beings are necessarily subject to suffering. But the line that would delineate natural or tolerable suffering from gratuitous, debilitating suffering is difficult to find. Once human suffering is possible, nothing restricts its range so that the kindest, or the weakest, or the most admirable people will be magically protected from it. Nothing limits suffering, in its intensity, from driving people to despair through grief, pain, or cruelty. Once suffering is posited as an essential component of human existence, radical suffering threatens every person. No one is protected from suffering that is so terrible that it breaks the spirit. No one can be guaranteed to be forever free from insane or sadistic powers: never to be tortured, abused, raped, starved, or persecuted beyond the bounds of what he or she is able to endure. Nor can many people retain hope in the face of drudgeries that sap and numb the vitality of the human spirit.

Suffering is a natural component of embodied, historical existence. But no mechanism can prevent natural pain and conflict from degenerating into radical suffering. A tragic environment to human freedom is suggested by the threat of suffering and radical suffering that is embedded in the conditions of human existence.

Freedom

Freedom, like Aristotle's reason or Hegel's *Geist,* is a way of expressing the constellation of capacities that are most distinctively human. Freedom describes that about human beings which cannot be reduced to biological drives or sociological forces. It is that power which enables human beings to enjoy beauty, to experience obligation and compassion, to care for friends and family, to strive for intellectual excellence, to participate in political systems, and so on. The inevitability of conflict and suffering circumscribes freedom, just as the curse on Oedipus's house sabotaged his actions. But freedom is fragile not only because of its tragic context but also because of an interior unsteadiness caused by anxiety and desire.

Anxiety is an apprehension of danger and a dread of the future. War can be feared, an operation dreaded, an execution faced with courage. Anxiety grasps these and other events only as vague possibilities. The future is filled with novelties and chances to succeed. But it conceals the darkness of pain and loss and ultimately the strange mystery of death. The indeterminateness of human life is the arena of freedom and responsibility, but it is also a crushing uncertainty. In times of social upheaval and disorder (like our own), when the future has little continuity with the past or present, anxiety at a cultural level increases. This is an exaggeration of a queasiness about the future that seems to be a perennial component of our existence.

Freedom has a necessary and internal connection to anxiety. Freedom propels human beings into an unknown future. Through desired projects and anticipations, through responsibilities accepted or forgotten, the emptiness of the future is engaged. Freedom gives a degree of form to the void.

Fragility enters through this connection between freedom and anxiety. Anxiety sickens freedom with an unpleasant suspicion that possibility is a code word for nothingness. Anxiety is the apprehension of the future less as a tempting promise for happiness than as a concealed threat. It is that interior disquiet that accompanies contingency. The willingness to be beguiled by sin or to succumb to despair begins when anxiety weakens freedom with auguries of failure.

A second element of human fragility is desire. Human beings do not experience themselves as complete or fulfilled. A perennial restlessness and yearning dogs our steps. Human beings are constituted by desire. Desire should not imply only selfish longing for personal satisfaction. It is also a faculty that permits human beings to orient themselves toward various goods such as beauty or family or work. Nonetheless, desire accentuates the fragility and unsteadiness of freedom.

It is the nature of desire to be in principle unfulfillable. "The feeling of disappointment, which always goes with satisfaction . . . is the index of a desire embodied in determined goals but never exhausted by these goals and their successes."[21] There never comes a time when I have everything I desire. There is no job, no security, no affection, not even an enlightenment that would so perfectly satisfy and complete me that nothing more could be desired. If nothing else, I would continue to desire the well-being of others. Further, no concrete desire ever perfectly coincides with its possible fulfillment. My love for my husband, however intense and delightful, does not exhaust my desire to love and to be loved. Finally, the content of desire is ambiguous. People long for spiritual happiness, but they also would like a good meal. People desire private satisfactions as well as affection and respect. Happiness and pleasure are not in principle mutually exclusive, but neither do they exist in natural harmony. The restlessness and conflict in desire reinforce feelings of unease and dissatisfaction.

Human beings are caught between opposing forces, conflicting desires, and between responsibilities and passions. Human beings are continuous with nature, composed of a particular genetic makeup, a protein pattern, biological drives for food and sex and security. They are conditioned by the culture, epoch, economic stratum, race, sex, and family in which they find themselves. Personal, social, and historical events act as elements of a determinism that constrains choices. Yet for all of these limitations, human beings are also responsible beings, longing for love and hungering after beauty.

Human beings are stretched apart between individuality and community, the desire for security and the exhilaration of joy and adventure. Less abstractly, the same creature who roams singles bars looking for quick satisfaction might entertain a sublime appreciation for poetry. Crass egocentric drives lie together with a passion for piety or love not only in the same species but in the same person. *Crime and Punishment's* Raskolnikov ax murders two old women one minute and the next he is so moved by pity that he gives his last ruble to a stranger.

The ambiguity and intensity of desire compel human beings to act in the midst of contending values and on the basis of ignorance and misunderstandings. Action under these circumstances is like a sailboat skimming along under heavy winds— but with a broken rudder. It does not require a prophetic genius to imagine the likelihood of disaster.

Anxiety and desire reflect perfections of the human spirit as in freedom it confronts a partly fixed and dangerous world, desiring affection, pleasure, and truth. But it is suffocating and intolerable to face contingency and death; it is unspeakable to bear the responsibility for ambiguous moral decisions; it is absurd to expect frail and sad human beings to be able to stand the yearning and antagonism to which desire subjects them.

> Hear my prayer, O LORD,
>   and give ear to my cry;
>   hold not thy peace at my tears!
> For I am thy passing guest,
>   a sojourner, like all my fathers.
> Look away from me, that I may know gladness,
>   before I depart and be no more!
> Psalm 39:12–13

Human beings are sojourners on the way to death, and the demands of life can be very tiring. It is often the case that freedom is more of a burden than a pleasure; we are enervated rather than exhilarated by the possibilities of life. It would be such a mercy, such a relief to hand freedom over to someone else. And so begins the eagerness to believe lies, to assent to whatever is easy and obvious, and to nurture indifference against the exhausting requirements of compassion. The harshness of anxiety and the restlessness of desire condemn freedom to betrayal and defeat. Freedom is the tragic flaw of human existence, at once the stamp of its greatness and its destruction.

Compassion

A tragic vision is branded by suffering, but the mark of tragedy is defiance rather than despair. The beginning of a tragic vision is anger and sorrow in the face of suffering. The horror of suffering provokes resistance. As such, it is an ethical (and ultimately theological) response to suffering: it begins and ends as compassion.

Compassion will be investigated in more detail in subsequent chapters. At this point, it is only necessary to suggest how it is that compassion survives the corruption of freedom by tragic conflict and fragility.

The capacity for compassion is contingent upon the ability to recognize the other person as human and as suffering. People are, however, more likely to encounter one another as representatives of some category than as actual human beings. One may feel pity or obligation toward another *person* but not toward "filthy Communist swine" or "lazy drug-addict welfare mothers." Compassion is the resuscitation of the *capacity* to recognize another person as human, possible even in the midst of a tragically structured environment.

Human beings are intersubjective and social creatures. Existence entails relationships with other people in work, political life, family life, and so on. If the capacity to recognize the other as human were destroyed, human life would be impossible. The ability to carry on a conversation or read a newspaper requires some ability to imaginatively comprehend the experience of other people, even those in situations very different from one's own. This is not a philosophical intuition of human "nature" or "essence." It is the immediate experience of being encountered by another person.

For example, sitting in the local bar with a group of friends, you notice that a young man has just hit his girlfriend very hard in the face and is about to do so again. You leap from your chair and dash over to stop him. Present in such a reaction is a prereflective, immediate understanding of the situation. A stranger is being unfairly attacked, and this is wrong. One need have no speculative knowledge of what human nature might consist in to understand what is going on. Further, one does not need to be equipped with any particular ethical theories, such as a sense of Duty Toward the Victimized. One need only grasp what is happening in order to experience a simple and spontaneous anger that this stranger is being mistreated. It is unnecessary to have been in this situation oneself. The bare awareness of being encountered by another human being is sufficient to urge one to stop the man from hitting her again. The entire event is a spontaneous understanding and response analogous to the feeling of being stung by an insect and swatting at it.

Compassionate understanding and response to suffering does not require the face-to-face immediacy of this example. The most general awareness of what a human being is suffices to evoke repugnance at descriptions of apartheid, starvation, or public indifference to AIDS patients.

A concern of much contemporary theology is to grant the dignity of specificity and uniqueness to people of different religions, races, ethnic backgrounds, and so on. This is an important attempt to resist the tacit imperialism of universal categories. The model of elitist Western rationalism can no longer be held up as a criterion for common humanity.

It still remains possible to feel pity and horror when a newspaper story relates the rape of an anonymous four-year-old child. Details as to the child's race, religion, or favorite color are not necessary to feel compassion for her suffering. Even after one has repudiated artificial norms of human nature, one is still obligated to understand and respond to suffering and injustice, wherever they occur.

For a tragic vision, ethical existence is based on the ability to spontaneously appreciate the humanity of another person and to desire her or his welfare. Moralism does not enable theology to transcend tragedy. Hester Prynne's treatment by the Puritans in Nathaniel Hawthorne's *The Scarlet Letter* exemplifies high-minded moralism combined with an utter lack of compassionate understanding. The mistreatment of homosexuals in this country is a modern example of this kind of hard-hearted moralism that has no roots in authentic ethical consciousness.

If normally intelligent people can understand a news story about a riot or a famine, then a compassionate response is possible. The *capacity* for ethical responsibility is present in the ability to understand personal or political disasters. The ability to perceive situations of suffering is not destroyed by tragedy. The opportunity to transcend tragedy is resident in the persistence of this capacity for recognizing and responding to suffering. Compassion is the resilience of the passion for justice that survives tragedy and in fact resists and defies it.

A tragic vision is no less relentless in its defiance of the causes of suffering than in its exposure of innocent, degrading suffering. The problem of evil is intensified by tragedy since it begins without any hope of justifying radical suffering. And yet the persistence of compassion within tragic vision may be a sign that this initial hopelessness need not lead to despair.

2

The Rupture of Creation

O my people, what have I done unto thee.
T. S. Eliot, "Ash Wednesday"

Tragedy explores evil by focusing on the kind of suffering that dehumanizes the sufferer and that cannot be understood as deserved. This chapter will argue that the recognition of the phenomenon of radical suffering will affect the way Christian theology understands the nature of evil and, correlatively, the goodness and power of God.

The evil in the book of Job is the injustice of his suffering, not his death. "And Job died, an old man, and full of days" (Job 42:17). When the prophet of Isaiah 65 envisions what redeemed life would look like, he describes human beings living out their lives unimpeded by war, poverty, calamity, violence, or early death. The prophet hopes for a time when:

> They shall build houses and inhabit them;
>   they shall plant vineyards and eat their fruit.
> They shall not build and another inhabit;
>   they shall not plant and another eat;
> for like the days of a tree shall the days of my people be,
>   and my chosen shall long enjoy the work of their hands.
> They shall not labor in vain,
>   or bear children for calamity.
>
> Isaiah 65: 21–23

Evil does not coincide with mortality; evil gratuitously hurts and disrupts human existence. Sin and radical suffering are

40

alike in that both cripple or destroy the possibilities for a fruit-
ful, peaceful existence. The list of what constitutes a happy
and redeemed life will undoubtedly vary from one person or
culture to the next. But however these goods are defined, sin
and radical suffering undermine capacities for enjoying dis-
tinctly human goods: for example, creating beauty, experiencing compassion and obligation, or being moved by wonder,
hope, or courage.

Creation is ephemeral and its beauty arises in conjunction
with the poignancy of its constant perishing. The beauty of the
natural world, even when it is accompanied by the real anguish
of pain and grief, expresses the goodness of what must inevitably pass away. There is sorrow here, but moral evil has not yet
encroached. Suffering itself is not synonymous with evil.

The destruction of the living human spirit does not parallel
the death that mortality brings to every creature. Evil is a
"sickness unto death," where the terror and horror is that the
person does not die but almost ceases to be human. Fackenheim quotes Primo Levi's description of this living death as
"the drowned . . . and anonymous mass . . . of non-men who
march and labour in silence, the divine spark dead within
them. . . . One hesitates to call them living: one hesitates to
call their death death."[1]

It is not necessarily evil that all human beings die, but it is
evil that the spark of life and dignity can be snuffed out in
them *before* they die. Sin and radical suffering prevent human
beings from pursuing their obligations or fulfillments. This by
itself is highly problematic. It means that the characteristic
form of human existence is such that guilt and pain incapaci-
tate it for a truly human life. But this evil is heightened when,
as argued in the preceding chapter, vulnerability to this kind of
destruction is contained in the conditions of human life.

It might be imagined that there is something fair about the
suffering of human beings if it could be successfully argued
that they had willingly betrayed access to a happy life by preferring evil to good. This, of course, is precisely how the myth
of the Fall accounts for the wretchedness of the human condition. But if the vulnerability of human beings to sin and suffering is an intrinsic liability of finitude, then the unhappy fate of
the human race is all the more difficult to justify.

A tragic context of human suffering does not negate the role of human guilt and responsibility. It places both sin and suffering within the broader situation of fragility. Sin and radical suffering are similar in that both are ways the human spirit can be broken. They are forms of evil rather than mortality because they prevent human beings from pursuing or even desiring the good. They are different from one another in that sin is a corruption of the human spirit by indifference to or desire for evil. In contrast, radical suffering is a kind of crippling of the human spirit by contingent and external forces. One is accountable for guilt in a way that one is not accountable for one's own suffering.

Sin

Sin is an evil in human existence because it undermines ethical relationships between individuals and in community life. The destructive power of sin occurs with particular viciousness at the level of corporate existence, especially as the chaos and destruction of injustice. The Hebrew prophets took sin with the utmost seriousness; they portray the righteous anger of God against sin in the strongest terms.

> The Lord has destroyed without mercy
>   all the habitations of Jacob;
> in his wrath he has broken down
>   the strongholds of the daughter of Judah;
> he has brought down to the ground in dishonor
>   the kingdom and its rulers.
>
> Lamentations 2:2

> So I will be to them like a lion,
>   like a leopard I will lurk beside the way.
> I will fall upon them like a bear robbed of her cubs,
>   I will tear open their breast,
> and there I will devour them like a lion,
>   as a wild beast would rend them.
>
> Hosea 13:7–8

The Christian tradition has also taken sin extremely seriously, as evidenced in the importance of the myth of the Fall and the doctrine of original sin. What about sin makes it so serious?

Sin is both a theological and an ethical category. Sin is against God, but the fundamental form of sin is cruelty and injustice toward God's creation.[2] The prophetic condemnation of sin attempts to show the inherently destructive dynamic of sin. Ethical obligations resonate with the created order. They express and mediate the relationship between humanity and God. To violate this order will have destructive consequences.

Sin is catastrophic because it introduces chaos and disharmony into history. The anonymous prophet of Isaiah 65 describes a moral order in which human beings live out their lives fruitfully and peaceably without violence. But if this moral order is ignored, there is no mechanism for assuring that only the evil will suffer. Chaos does not seek out individual sinners and chastise them appropriately. Chaos is death and destruction unleashed on an entire social system and, with the help of technology, upon the world itself.

In lamenting or predicting evil, the prophets often single out the suffering of the weakest and most helpless:

> Infants and babes faint
>   in the streets of the city.
> They cry to their mothers,
>   "Where is bread and wine?"
> as they faint like wounded men . . .
>   as their life is poured out. . . .
> In the dust of the streets
>   lie the young and the old;
> my maidens and my young men
>   have fallen by the sword.
>   Lamentations 2:11–12, 21

Suffering is scattered indiscriminately through the community and especially affects those who had least opportunity to perpetrate social injustice: children, nursing and pregnant mothers, young virgins, the very old, and the very poor. The prophets are not describing a strict correlation between sinners and their punishment but a destructive chaos rampant in an entire population.

Perhaps Israel "received from the LORD's hand double for all her sins" (Isa. 40:2), not because of the harsh zealousness of divine retribution, but because of the interior dynamic of sin itself. Sin introduces destructive powers into a community that do not necessarily coincide with the direct intentions of any human being. The ultimate explosion of folly and injustice into wanton violence need not reflect anything directly desired, and yet it is the consequence of sin all the same. Sin present in structural injustice is a power beyond individual wickedness or immorality. Sin is similar to tragedy in that it encompasses individual human actions in an already corrupted environment. But it is not simply tragic, it is moral. It is the willful repudiation of the stewardship that might have been the mark of humanity's relationship to God.

The destructive power of sin may be illuminated by looking at four of its dimensions: deception, callousness, bondage, and guilt. The vacillation of sin between guilt and bondage, between choice and destiny, and between the individual and the community will hopefully be preserved by maintaining a tension among these four features.

Deception

Because human beings are not typically overtly sadistic, they need to screen themselves from the destructive nature of their actions and desires. For this reason, deception may be the most ubiquitous feature of sin. In the myth of the Fall, it is by way of a lie that evil finds its way into the happy Garden of Eden. Deception involves a willingness to be beguiled by evil; it is the acceptance and approval of a lie. Sin does not require a self-conscious desire for evil as such. Deception is the mask evil wears to disguise its true nature and to make itself palatable to people who would be disturbed by concrete suffering.

Hannah Arendt describes the use of "language rules" by the Nazis, in which their genocidal policies were described by more tepid expressions: genocide became the much milder "final solution," murder became "evacuation" *(Aussiedlung)* or "special treatment" *(Sonderbehandlung)*. She observes that the expression "language rule" is itself a prevarication. The rigid "rules" were nothing other than carefully crafted lies. These lies were not intended to conceal what was being done: those initiated into the language rules were also initiated into the atrocities. The function of these language games was rather to prevent participants in genocide "from equating it with their old 'normal' knowledge of murder and lies."[3]

Deception does not necessarily conceal information but, rather, so encodes a situation that its reality is effectively obscured. The willingness to be deceived by lies does not necessarily indicate a desire for evil or a hard indifference to suffering; it might be as much a pain—a shame and an insecurity—that seeks alleviation, albeit in a cowardly way. But deception can also represent a more profound collusion with evil. It can be a defense that enables one to participate in great cruelties by pretending they are something else.

Self-deception testifies both to the incipient goodness of human beings and to the insidious power of sin. Self-deception is necessary because human beings are not typically so wicked that torture, murder, or starvation are matters of indifference. In order for people to pursue actions and policies that result in death and poverty, they must disguise their choices and shield themselves from explicit knowledge of the consequences of their actions.

Every desire, as Thomas Aquinas insisted, is for some good. A chemical company might poison a river by illegally dumping toxic wastes in order to cut down on expenses. They destroy the creatures in the river. Miscarriages and leukemia increase in the communities that get their water from the river. The object of desire was not death and destruction to various forms of life: the desired thing was a certain profit margin. Financial security is not evil, but the idea that whatever is done to promote wealth is good has certain ethical problems. Deception inserts itself between the penultimate good of a healthy business and the decision to dump toxic wastes. People in the company might be ashamed to say baldly that pollution, miscarriages, and cancer were small prices (for someone else to pay) in order for them to become fabulously well-to-do. To disguise the fact that their actions presuppose precisely this assumption, they cloud their reasoning with lies. The river will not be badly damaged; the FDA has not determined the level of exposure required to get cancer from this chemical; the economic health of the country depends on the financial well-being of our company, etc.

Prevarication gives sin enormous power for destruction. Precisely because evil is clothed in admirable words and pictures, it is not recognized and confronted. Martin Luther's metaphor for evil disguised as good—"white Satan"—evokes both the beguiling loveliness of evil and its terrible danger. When people acquiesce to lies, evil is particularly potent. Deception disguises sin and frees it to function more efficiently. It blinds human beings to their obligations and to the reality of their situation. Sin in the form of deception enervates moral consciousness and begins the dehumanizing process of crippling ethical existence.

Callousness

A second dimension of sin is callousness. The capacity to recognize and respond to other human beings is intrinsic to human consciousness. But sin replaces the spontaneous pity for those who suffer with indifference, with an apathy that cannot be moved by another's sorrow. Callousness represents a deeper level of sin. It is less necessary to disguise evil because the capacity to recognize it as evil has been diminished. It should be noted that these dimensions of sin are not unrelated archaeological strata but integrated aspects of the human capacity for evil. For example, when one accepts certain lies about the inferiority of a race or sex as true, it is easier to nurture indifference toward suffering caused by racism or sexism.

Isak Dinesen relates the following event that occurred when she was living in Africa. Two white men visiting a friend at his farm stood by, casually chatting, while a black teenager who worked for the farmer was flogged for about a quarter of an hour. He had "talked back" to his employer. The young man died during the night.[4] These two farmers were not sadistic criminals. They were normal, law-abiding citizens. Yet they were capable of standing by, watching a young man tortured to death before their eyes with no more interest than they might expend on a flock of starlings sitting on a fence.

The capacity to watch someone tortured to death without registering much interest, let alone horror, witnesses to a serious degree of damage to the spontaneous "animal pity by which all normal men are affected in the presence of physical suffering."[5] The presence of this callousness—not in criminals or psychopaths but in upstanding citizens—attests to the damage that sin effects in a community at large. Fackenheim suggests that one of the things that makes the Nazi Holocaust unique is that it was not perpetrated by sadists or the insane but by "ordinary jobholders."[6] At least in this one respect, the evil of the Holocaust is continuous with most other evils that infect human communities. The danger of sin lies here: the

callousness that makes terrible cruelties possible is not per-
ceived to be an aberration. Callousness is not present in a community through a handful of criminals but as a characteristic
of the community itself. The community mediates attitudes
and values that make violence and cruelty normal.

Like deception, callousness suggests both a fragment of good
left in human beings and the ever more profound efficacy of
sin. Typically, callousness does not completely eliminate the
capacity for "animal pity." Rather, pity is extended to a nar-
rowly defined normative group and excludes all others. In a
patriarchal society the normativeness of maleness makes the
humanity of women marginal. Men who are brought up by loving mothers, married to wives they respect, and who raise
young daughters with tender affection can be so infected by the
sinful callousness of their culture that they are apparently incapable of recognizing women as fellow human beings. Lies
and callousness operate at such a deep level of consciousness
that they prevent the eyes from seeing what is before them.

> In 1973, hundreds of children were sent away from their parents in
> Johannesburg back to some homeland. . . . A reporter of one of
> the English-speaking newspapers asked the Bantu Administra-
> tion Board, "Why are you doing this? These are children you are
> sending away from their parents." The white officer in charge of
> this operation said, "Well, you know, you must try to understand
> that these black women are not the same as our women. They
> really do not feel bad when we send their children away, because,
> you see, they do not see things the same way as we do. They are
> really very happy when we relieve them of the burden of having to
> care for their children so that they can work uninterruptedly for
> the white madams they work for."[7]

Lies and callous indifference conspire to enable an ordinary bu-
reaucrat to carry out a policy that otherwise would have been
considered outrageously cruel. The basic capacity to see suffering and injustice and to spontaneously loathe and resist them
has been limited to a select group but not numbed into non-
existence. On the one hand, callousness has not completely destroyed the desire for justice or the capacity for pity; that is why
human beings can be held accountable for their apathy. On the
other hand, indifference to at least certain groups within a society is a "normal" part of a community's life together; it, like
deception, disguises evil and so gives it greater power.

Bondage

Sin as deception and as callousness are present both through individuals and through economic, religious, political, and social structures. It would be misleading to suggest that socialization in a racist society causally determines an individual to participate in a lynching. It would be equally misleading to say that racism is located only in the isolated acts of racist individuals and is not mediated by law, religion, language, by the entire web of invisible interactions that constitute a community.

The mediation of sin both by individuals and by more complex social structures illuminates the dialectic between bondage and guilt. Sin understood as socialization (the modern term for Fate) withholds from human existence ethical responsibility altogether; sin understood as unfettered free choice is a kind of Pelagianism that fails to acknowledge the engagement of individuals in broader systems. An interaction between guilt and bondage gives to sin its paradoxical character. This section will describe sin as bondage; the next one will illustrate how sin nonetheless entails guilt.

Sin damages human beings and communities by diminishing their capacity to perceive injustice, to experience compassion, and to discern right from wrong. People participate in the process through which they are dehumanized by evil, acquiescing to it, accepting it. And yet this participation is not typically an explicit, self-conscious desire for evil or enjoyment of cruelty. Deception and callousness limit the capacity of human beings to understand the ethical dimensions of their experience, to feel compassion for suffering or anger at injustice. This limitation occurs prior to any particular choice or perception: the reality one sees and responds to is already shaped by lies and indifference. Sin distorts the situation to which one reacts and numbs the feelings of right and wrong. The two white farmers in Isak Dinesen's story were unable to see that a young man was being tortured to death in front of them or to feel outrage at his murder. The situation was veiled and twisted by racist assumptions and lies.

Oedipus was ignorant of his true position, Antigone was torn by mutually exclusive obligations. In both cases responsibility was limited by circumstances outside the hero's control. This is the characteristic way sin functions: it corrupts the environment in which human beings must act and deceives them about their real situation. The sin of sexism has become so deeply embedded in our society that even actions to resist it become drawn into its destructive pattern. Efforts to enable women to participate more fully in work outside of the home often are couched in language that implies that raising children or keeping house are degrading and inferior activities. For women who find these activities rewarding, creative, or merely necessary, feminism can be as offensive and painful as patriarchy. The very attempt to overcome the devaluation of women can have the effect of perpetuating it in a new guise.

Sin so deeply infects a community that every action is tainted and corrupt. Deception and callousness cripple the capacity for ethical existence. Further, the context of action is already fractured by sin and draws even the desire for good into itself. Sin becomes a kind of bondage that entangles human beings and communities even before they choose or desire evil.

The ransom theory of atonement gives a mythic/poetic expression to the bondage of the human race: Satan *owns* the human race after the unpleasantness in the Garden of Eden. Adam and Eve were beguiled by his lie, and they are now his rightful property. God is, so to speak, grief-stricken at the loss of the human race but bound by the Law that gives Satan rightful ownership of sinners. God cannot override this Law, but neither is God content to leave humanity in thralldom to Satan. God sends the Son to earth. As divine, Jesus is sinless, but as human, he is subject to Satan. Satan is so excited about getting his hands on the Son of God, now vulnerable to him in human form, that he is simply beside himself. The Son is crucified. But in his enthusiasm, Satan forgot that only sinners were his rightful property. By killing the sinless one, he forfeits his right to sinners. Through Jesus's death, the human race is ransomed from slavery to sin.

In this story, the *problem* of sin is bondage more than guilt. Human beings are trapped by lies more than perverted by wickedness. They are simultaneously evil's perpetrators and its victims. According to the ransom theory, this ambiguity in sin permits human beings to be the objects of divine pity rather than of condemnation. Bondage is not fate that removes responsibility from human beings, but it places sin within a tragic context.

Guilt

These first three dimensions of sin indicate that it is not necessarily an explicit desire for evil. Evil comes through human choices, desires, and policies, but the evil that is achieved is not always that which was directly desired. However willing Germany was to be seduced by Hitler's visions of a Third Reich and however much the long history of antisemitism made them indifferent to *Kristallnacht,* it is difficult to imagine that millions of German bakers and secretaries explicitly *desired* the unspeakable atrocities of Buchenwald and Auschwitz. It is the power of evil to insinuate itself into history through kind-hearted, normal people that makes it so appalling.

Human action is located in an already corrupted environment. To this extent, sin can be understood as having a tragic dimension. But corruption and fragility do not have the effect of destroying human responsibility. The capacity to understand another's suffering and to conceive of justice remains. Sin is an ethical category that reflects a fundamental character of human existence as relational and entailing obligation. The failure to recognize and respond to the other as human or as suffering is culpable. Human beings are responsible for what they do and are not simply passive victims of original sin, corrupt social institutions, or deceptive language games. In the midst of these determinations, human beings remain responsible agents. The tragic context of sin does not coerce a drug-runner into shooting a competitor; nor is a religious community forced by demonic powers to exclude women from positions of leadership. Sin requires assent at some level to lies, callousness, and cruelty. Consent to evil represents the transition from tragedy and bondage to guilt.

The cruelty that is inflicted by individuals and by social systems is something for which human beings can be properly held accountable: cruelty and oppression are not simply footprints of the Fates. Sin is the betrayal of obligations rooted in the relationships that exist among human beings. It is possible for people to mind when another person suffers. It is possible for human beings to want to know the truth and to feel unsatisfied with propaganda and consoling fictions. Indifference to suffering cannot be explained by appeal to society's assumptions, however much these shape human beings. Criminals are held accountable for their crimes. So much more should "good citizens" be liable for their indifference, greed, and self-deception that make injustice so palatable and cruelty so much more natural than kindness.

It is the dignity of human beings to exist ethically, with obligations toward one another and toward society; the *imago Dei* may be glimpsed in the compassion people can feel toward one another. Betrayal of this dignity and responsibility requires the collusion between desire and sin.

Human beings are dehumanized by sin: the evil effected by sin is not identical with what people may desire. And yet this tragic dimension should not conceal the guilt human beings bear for their hard hearts. Sin is a corruption caused by a tacit or explicit acceptance of evil. Human beings are crippled and broken because they encumber themselves with guilt.

Suffering

All mortal creatures are subject to pain and loss. In addition to these kinds of suffering, human beings are vulnerable to a kind of suffering that is degrading and dehumanizing. Capacities for affection, enjoyment, hope, and desire are eroded by radical suffering.

The phenomenon of undeserved, destructive suffering is not acknowledged by most classical theologians; its recognition poses problems for theodicy that apparently did not exist for Augustine, Thomas Aquinas, or Calvin. In much of the classical theological tradition, the problem of human suffering is obscured by the tradition's focus on sin as the primary expression of evil. Theodicy addressed the question of why *sin* was permitted to introduce evil into an otherwise good creation and what God does to redeem humanity from its guilt.

Contemporary theology is much more willing to acknowledge the injustice of some kinds of suffering. But sensitivity to injustice and suffering often becomes a new dualism that categorizes human beings according to membership in the group of the oppressed or the oppressors. Dorothee Soelle writes: "In the face of suffering you are either with the victim or the executioner—there is no other option."[8]

I am not convinced that this objectification of humanity into victim and executioner does justice to the complexity of the human individual or to the dynamic of evil. The black man who is victimized by a racist society may beat his wife and rape his daughter. The middle-class housewife depends for her standard of living on the oppression of third-world workers. But she may spend her days volunteering at a residence for battered women and typing newsletters advocating justice in Central America. The web that unites victim and tyrant in the same person is more complex than the white hat/black hat caricature that seems banal even in its natural habitat, the "grade B" movie. Further, the portrayal of victims of suffering as entirely passive does not seem entirely appropriate. Presenting images of pathetic, helpless victims does little to restore dignity to those who suffer; it may be closer to paternalism than real compassion.

The exploration of the problem of evil must resist the temptation to absorb the problem of suffering into guilt and sin. It must also avoid the more contemporary temptation to resort to moral dualisms. Both temptations can be enormously satisfying: they help take some of the sting out of the idea of suffering. However pitiable the sufferers are, at least it is comforting to remember that they are being punished or purged of their sin. The sheer horror of hopeless suffering becomes more bearable when accompanied by righteous anger; despair is replaced by hatred of the oppressors.

A tragic vision cannot permit itself to resort to such consolations. The raw reality of suffering must be encountered without the aid of false dualism, excuses, or justifications. The two faces of human evil, sin and suffering, must be permitted to emerge in their distinctiveness. But the translation of this duality in the nature of evil into actual human beings should be avoided. The objectification of human beings in any form, including as oppressor or victim, denudes them of their humanity. A category, a statistic replaces the depth and complexity of the human person. Both the obscenity of evil and the hope for redemption are concealed when categories and concepts replace human beings. Although theology is by its nature an abstract and conceptual exercise, we cannot allow ourselves to forget that the reality of evil is not present in ideas but is borne by the fragile bodies of utterly unique persons existing in concrete situations of ambiguity, pain, and betrayal.

Radical Suffering vs. Suffering

Rebecca Chopp argues that the massive suffering of humanity has a "nonidentity" character to it: it resists expression in theory. It cannot be resolved into any meaning. It is precisely this massive, meaningless suffering that must be thematized as the central problem of contemporary theology:

> The nonidentity character of suffering means that suffering cannot be forgotten or ignored in history's interpretation or construction; once progress has shoved the masses of humanity onto life's margins, history is broken, its end forever in question, and its purpose lost in suspension.[9]

The immense and intense suffering caused by oppression, injustice, and political violence challenges the meaningfulness of history and of Christianity. Radical suffering represents another dimension of suffering that intensifies the challenge suffering presents to Christian thought. It should be emphasized that this turning from suffering caused by injustice to radical suffering is intended to *augment* sensitivity to the importance of suffering in contemporary theology and is not intended to criticize or replace Jewish or liberation theology's emphasis on the social and political genesis of suffering. The illumination of the power of suffering to destroy human beings may permit the radicality of the evil of suffering to be seen more clearly.

Radical suffering is present when the negativity of a situation is experienced as an assault on one's personhood *as such*. Such an assault is distinguished from the pain an athlete might feel when she subjects herself to difficult training. For her the pain is secondary to the enjoyment of competition. It also contrasts with the situation of people who suffer very terribly but whose suffering moves them to new heights of compassion and courage. There are experiences of suffering that are necessary to achieve some desired good or that deepen one's sensitivity to others or bring one to a greater maturity and understanding. And then some kinds of suffering can be reasonably said to be deserved, as when a murderer is put in prison. Radical suffering is a phenomenon that is different from all of these experiences of suffering.

Radical suffering assaults and degrades that about a person which makes her or him most human. This assault reduces the capacity of the sufferer to exercise freedom, to feel affection, to

hope, to love God. Radical suffering pinches the spirit of the
sufferer, numbing it and diminishing its range. The distinctiveness of radical suffering does not lie in its intensity or its
injustice but in its power over the sufferer.

Radical suffering is often caused by dehumanizing treatment
at the hands of another person. *Sybil* told the story of a woman
who developed seventeen personalities as a mechanism to protect herself from the brutality of her mother. Years of torment
and abuse at the hands of her mother literally drove her insane.[10] Someone who is broken by years of imprisonment and
torture would provide another example. It is also possible for
someone to be dehumanized by grief, sickness, or injury.

D. H. Lawrence describes the gradual diminishment of the
personhood of Clifford Chatterley. Clifford becomes a dead, almost mechanized creature because of the physically and spiri-
tually paralyzing injury he suffered in World War I.[11]

Social systems can be created to dehumanize human beings
without necessarily killing them. South Africa's apartheid
system is organized on the principle that some people are sub-
human. A dehumanizing social system seeks to strip the
humanity of its participants, making the struggle for self-
respect a superhuman task.

The Nazi death camps were a demonically hyperbolic expression of a social system designed to destroy the human
spirit. It was insufficient "merely" to eradicate the Jewish population. The Nazi logic of destruction included not only mass
murder, but the attempt to "produce in the victim a 'self-
disgust' to the point of wanting death or even committing suicide. And this—nothing less—was the essential goal. The Nazi
logic of destruction was aimed, ultimately, at the victim's *self-*
destruction."[12] The camps were designed to effect this end, as
Pelagia Lewinska, a survivor of the camps, relates:

> At the outset the living places, the ditches, the mud, the piles of
> excrement . . . had appalled me with their horrible filth. . . . And
> then I saw the light! I saw that it was not a question of disorder
> . . . but that, on the contrary, a very thoroughly considered con-
> scious idea was in the back of the camp's existence. They had
> condemned us to die in our own filth, to drown in mud, in our
> own excrement. They wished to abase us, to destroy our human
> dignity, to efface every vestige of humanity . . . to fill us with
> horror and contempt toward ourselves and our fellows.[13]

Radical suffering is accompanied by an experience of abasement that destroys one's basic human dignity. Anguish effaces the very humanity of the sufferer and in this way cripples her ability to defend herself. A self-loathing or despair enervates even the indignation that would make one realize that one had been wronged. The most extreme violence against the human being is that it can create a soul incapable of self-defense because the spark of self-respect or dignity has been snuffed out by humiliation and pain.

Emmanuel Levinas compares Socrates's death with this living death of the human person. Socrates died a good, if unjust, death. He died heroically.

> Yet we know that the possibilities of tyranny are much more extensive. . . . It can exterminate in the tyrannized soul even the very capacity to be struck. . . . To have a servile soul is to be incapable of being jarred, incapable of being ordered. . . . Fear fills the soul to such an extent that one no longer sees it, but sees from its perspective.[14]

The heroism of martyrdom and the defiance of tragic heroes testify to the injustice of a world order in which the good are defeated by the wicked or the strong. But they simultaneously testify to an order of justice that transcends their defeat. In radical suffering the soul itself has been so crippled that it can no longer defy evil. The destruction of the human being is so complete that even the shred of dignity that might demand vindication is extinguished.

The Destructiveness of Radical Suffering

The most characteristic feature of radical suffering is that it is self-destructive: the following analysis exposes the dynamic that gives to suffering its destructive power.

Radical suffering is accompanied by a sense of contingency. It is distinct from the general consciousness of pain and death. It may be that I am perfectly aware that my body is vulnerable to injury, but this knowledge does not prepare me to face life as a quadriplegic when I am hit by a drunk driver or by a bomb. Or to take an example from Alice Walker's *The Color Purple:* "When the neighbors brought her husband's body home, it had been mutilated and burnt. The sight of it nearly killed her. . . .

Although the widow's body recovered, her mind was never the same."[15] It may be that I am reconciled to the fact that I live in a racist society, but I can still be undone when my husband's body is brought home to me from a lynching tree.

Radical suffering is concrete and contextual. It arises out of the particularity of a situation and is experienced through personal immediacy. Suffering occasioned by poverty, oppression, sexism—as much as by loss or sickness—is always and irreducibly my own. Even if my suffering is explicitly as a member of a community, the experience of it remains uniquely mine and cannot be absorbed into the larger whole. The suffering of a starving Bolivian woman is different from that of an unemployed German steelworker or a Laotian political prisoner. Further, any given starving Bolivian woman will experience poverty and hunger within her own context and personal resources. She is not simply a statistic of world hunger but an utterly unique event of suffering. She may or may not find resources to resist the plunge into radical suffering.

Suffering's concreteness also occurs within the matrix of familial, cultural, political, and economic relations. Radical suffering is not a generic essence but is shaped by its context. "Starvation varies in the context of a POW camp, slum, hospital, or olympic training camp."[16] It affects individuals as they are met with a particular event or situation. Each experience of suffering will be individual and shaped by its context. The resources of the person and the situation will differ, making every example of suffering unique. Radical suffering still remains recognizable as destructive and unjust, whatever its guise.

The power to resist suffering distinguishes meaningful suffering from radical suffering. As long as suffering can be resisted, only death will overcome the sufferer; resistance replaces the final degradation of radical suffering.

Suffering can be resisted in two ways. The first occurs when the conditions that cause suffering are identified and defied. The mothers of the Plaza de Mayo in Argentina protesting the "disappearance" of their children, civil rights workers in this country, or the fighters in the Warsaw ghetto during World War II provide examples. This dangerous work of resistance reveals a transcendence of the immediacy of suffering that makes it possible to imagine and to labor for an alternative. When for practical or psychological reasons it becomes impossible to resist the conditions of suffering, one is delivered to a situation over which one has little control.

The second form of resistance emerges when no practical change can be anticipated. The cancer is incurable, the prison impenetrable, the situation hopeless. Even under these conditions, it is possible to prevent suffering from degrading and destroying one's very humanity. Pelagia Lewinska, continuing her description of the death camps, remembers that she felt "under orders to live" precisely when she realized that the aim of the camp was not only to kill her but to dehumanize her in the process. "And if I did die in Auschwitz, it would be as a human being, I would hold on to my dignity. . . . And a terrible struggle began which went on day and night."[17]

Gabriel Marcel contrasts hope with despair in a context where freedom from suffering cannot be anticipated. When real change is impossible, resistance is the refusal to accept "the inner determinism . . . threatening when the trial is upon me to change me into one of those degraded, abnormal and . . . hypnotized expressions of human personality produced by despair."[18] In any situation of "humiliation, torture, and murder, the maintenance by the victims of a shred of humanity is not merely the basis of resistance but already a part of it."[19]

Radical suffering arises when the power to resist in one or both of these senses is absent. It might be inferred that because there are examples of people facing hopeless situations who maintain their humanity, that those who succumb to despair have no one to blame but themselves. It is true that radical suffering has an element of self-destruction in it. Simone Weil describes the participation of the soul in its own destruction:

> In anyone who has suffered affliction for a long enough time there is a complicity with regard to his own affliction. This complicity impedes all the efforts he might make to improve his lot; it goes so far as to prevent him from seeking a way of deliverance. . . . Even a person who has come through his affliction will still have something left in him compelling him to plunge into it again, if it has bitten deeply and forever into the substance of his soul. It is as though affliction had established itself in him like a parasite and were directing him to suit its own purposes.[20]

It is not unusual for people to respond to victims of radical suffering with disgust and to blame them for what happened. A sour-smelling street person hardly seems human; he or she is more likely to inspire revulsion than pity. The sign of radical suffering is that the person is made inhuman by suffering. The strangeness of such persons places them beyond the pale. But the complicity of the self in its own destruction does not parallel the culpability of sin. The absence of even the desire for freedom from pain makes plain the hideous damage that suffering can do to the human spirit. Persons who are so badly hurt that they become accomplices in their own destruction, far from sharing responsibility for their defeat, are persons already broken by pain. Part of the terrible guilt borne by the victimizer lies in cruelty's power not only to hurt people but literally to destroy them. The responsibility borne by the perpetrator of evil is not shared by the victim. Emil Fackenheim points out that in the face of this kind of destruction little beyond grief for the victims and horror at their tormentors is possible:

> Nor can [anyone], without gratuitous, posthumous insult to all the *Muselmänner,* ask about even one why he let himself be reduced to a state of death while still alive. And, rather than be quick to raise the question of resistance, one may well ask how one can raise it at all.[21]

Radical suffering defines the human being as a victim or sufferer, so she (or he) becomes a deformed creature whose *habitus* is suffering. All experience is absorbed into suffering and the sufferer is impaled upon her pain. The past is gone and the future a miserable repetition of the present. J. R. R. Tolkien describes the last leg of Frodo's quest in the land of shadow in this way. His friend and companion, Sam, tries to encourage him with memories of the past, but Frodo cannot remember them: "At least, I know that such things happened, but I cannot see them. No taste of food, no feel of water, no sound of wind, no memory of tree or grass or flower, no image of moon or star are left to me. I am naked in the dark, Sam, and there is no veil between me and the wheel of fire. I begin to see it even with my waking eyes, and all else fades."[22] In radical suffering there is no veil between the sufferer and an abyss of pain and meaninglessness—"all else fades."

Radical suffering is the incurable wound of despair that annihilates the future, severs relationship, and withholds from suffering any possible meaning. Radical suffering penetrates through the whole person and leaves only a dehumanized rag of a self behind. Augustine nominated despair as a likely candidate for the "unforgivable sin." While this appears somewhat hard-hearted, the logic is clear. Evil can be repented of and forgiven, suffering might become the occasion of redemption or provoke a community to resist injustice. But in despair there is no hope; one has been maimed beyond recovery. The human being is put beyond the pale of redemption—not because of guilt but as a victim of suffering.

Spirits can be destroyed just as bones can be broken and bodies killed. Human beings can be subjected to such pain that they are crushed rather than redeemed by it. This introduces into the problem of evil a surd more terrible even than sin or suffering. As Simone Weil writes:

> The great enigma of human life is not suffering but affliction. It is not surprising that the innocent are killed, tortured, driven from their country, made destitute, or reduced to slavery, imprisoned in camps or cells, since there are criminals to perform such actions. It is not surprising either that disease is the cause of long sufferings, which paralyze life and make it into an image of death, since nature is at the mercy of the blind play of mechanical necessities. But it *is* surprising that God should have given affliction the power to seize the very souls of the innocent and to take possession of them as their sovereign lord. At the very best, he who is branded by affliction will keep only half his soul.[23]

Radical Suffering and Theodicy

The several strands of tragic vision must come together now to restate the problem of evil that haunts theology and faith. These strands will be connected as follows: first, the goodness of creation; second, its tragic structure; third, the rupture of creation by evil in the forms of suffering and sin.

Created Goodness

Genesis assures us that when God created, God considered the world to be very good. The world is beautiful. It provides what no amount of divine contemplation could: the infinitely various, lovely fecundity of concrete existence. The Bible has

the temerity to suggest that the beauty of creation adds to
God's enjoyment:

> Thou makest springs gush forth in the valleys;
>   they flow between the hills,
> they give drink to every beast of the field;
>   the wild asses quench their thirst. . . .
> The trees of the LORD are watered abundantly,
>   the cedars of Lebanon which he planted.
> In them the birds build their nests;
>   the stork has her home in the fir trees.
> The high mountains are for the wild goats;
>   the rocks are a refuge for the badgers. . . .
> The young lions roar for their prey,
>   seeking their food from God. . . .
> May the glory of the LORD endure for ever,
>   may the LORD rejoice in his works.
>   Psalm 104:10–11, 16–18, 21, 31

Human beings, with their gift of freedom, add another dimension to creation. Through them beauty might be augmented by love given and received. A tender desire between
God and God's people gives a fire of joy beyond the delight of
beauty to creation. People are called to work with God, to bring
the goodness of creation to ever deeper and fuller expression.

The perfection of creation requires this work between God
and human beings. The loveliness of the cosmos, the courage of
a good woman, the delight between lovers cannot exist only in
God's mind, they must come to expression in the alien reality of
finitude. Tragic vision shares with the Bible a sense of the wonder of creation; the vitality of finite existence introduces a good
that cannot be accomplished by the self-contemplation of Aristotle's Unmoved Mover.

Tragic Structure

The good of creation comes from the fact that something
other than God is granted the gift of existence. But what is
other than God cannot share the unchanging serenity of love or
the endless youth of eternity or the harmonious unity of the
divine life. The beauty of the world lies in its variety and diversity. Yet conflict will inevitably arise as the multitude of creatures pursue opposing ends. Tigers will prey on young gazelles.

Ice ages will waste entire populations and ecosystems. Agriculture will beat back the jungle. From these conflicts, sorrows, and losses emerges the fierce beauty of creation. Sorrow must accompany beauty, but it need not overthrow the poignant loveliness of nature. Creation is tragically structured, but tragedy is neither the barrenness of nothingness nor the wickedness of evil. Tragedy is the price paid for existence—but the fecund grace of nature makes it appear that the price is not too high.

Not only creation, but freedom, too, is tragically structured. The conditions under which human freedom must exist are tragic in the sense that responsibility finds itself limited by ignorance and conflict, by deception and callousness. The tragic structure of freedom lies not only in its restriction but also in its fragility. Human beings are chattel to anxiety, ambiguity, and restless desire. They must seek the good while surrounded by a thousand dangers, uncertainties, and conflicts. People are born into societies already fractured by racism, poverty, drug-addiction, and misogyny. The conditions under which human beings must live are already corrupted by evil and are too painful to be borne. Freedom to love, to sorrow with compassion, to become intoxicated by beauty betrays itself. "I have set before you life and death, . . . choose life" (Deut. 30:19). But human beings are unable to do so; we choose death. Conflict and fragility overwhelm us. In an impenetrable mystery of freedom and tragedy, evil infects the human race.

Rupture of Creation

Suffering and sorrow are present to all human life without necessarily obscuring the goodness of creation. But the destructive power of radical suffering rips the mask of beauty and wonder off of the face of creation. A hideous, gaping sore is revealed in the very midst of life. Radical suffering is a malignancy that distorts the whole of history, poisoning it at its very root. Alex Haley, in *Roots,* describes such suffering:

> Kunta stood there wild-eyed, his body shaking, his brain flashing a memory of toubob faces in the wood grove, on the big canoe, in the prison, in the place where he had been sold, on the heathen farm, in the woods where he had been caught, beaten,

lashed, and shot three times before. . . . He knew from their faces
he would die now, and he didn't care. . . . Wrestling him vio-
lently towards a tree, they tore the clothes off him and tied him
tightly to it around the middle of his body. He steeled himself to
be beaten to death. But then the bleeding toubob halted ab-
ruptly, and a strange look came onto his face, almost a smile, and
he spoke briefly, hoarsely to the younger one. . . . Then he
pointed to Kunta's foot, and then to the ax in his hand. . . .
Kunta was screaming and thrashing as the ax flashed up, then
down so fast—severing skin, tendons, muscles, bone—that
Kunta actually heard the ax thud into the trunk as the shock of
it sent the agony deep into his brain. As the explosion of pain
bolted through him, Kunta's upper body spasmed forward and
his hands went flailing downward as if to save the front half of
his foot, which was falling forward, as bright red blood jetted
from the stump as he plunged into blackness.[24]

If an event such as this occurred only once in the entire
history of the human race, it would mar and tear the very fabric
of the created order. But it has happened millions of times, it
continues to happen, and there is no sign that it will stop in
the future. The litany of human crimes and anguish is without
end; it stretches from the dawn of our race, it covers every
continent and every epoch. People not brutalized by racism or
starvation are paralyzed by meaninglessness or deadened by
dehumanizing work. A gay man is beaten senseless by a band
of macho toughs; a middle-class woman is driven to suicide by
a bad marriage and an undiagnosed case of manic-depressive
psychosis. No class or sex or country is free from the destructive power of suffering and sin. It enervates business people,
cripples workers, destroys prisoners. Human beings are violated day and night, as individuals, in communities, as a race.
The suffering of humanity is not only a tragedy, it is a *rupture*
of creation; through it the world is defiled.

> Yet, O LORD, thou art our Father;
>   we are the clay, and thou art our potter;
>   we are all the work of thy hand . . . .
>   Behold, consider, we are all thy people.
> Thy holy cities have become a wilderness,
>   Zion has become a wilderness,
>   Jerusalem a desolation.

Our holy and beautiful house,
  where our fathers praised thee,
has been burned by fire,
  and all our pleasant places have become ruins.
Wilt thou restrain thyself at these things, O LORD?
Wilt thou keep silent, and afflict us sorely?
                                        Isaiah 64:8–12

It seems God creates human beings only for death and destruction, for degradation and pain. The very conditions that give the human race existence bring it intolerable suffering. Whatever share of the burden of responsibility we must bear, the immensity of suffering negates collective guilt and reveals the injustice of our situation.

Human beings are crippled by sin and become capable of performing and permitting the most wicked acts of cruelty and injustice. When human beings are degraded by sin, new forms of suffering are added to natural mortality: misogyny, death camps, and slavery—demonic mockeries of human freedom and beauty. Sin and suffering testify to a fundamental cleavage and brokenness that is at the heart of human life. The screams of children and the silence of despair cannot be drowned out by theodicies or justified by the cosmic wonder of nature. *Even the death of a Messiah cannot atone for the anguish of the world.*

If the disease that crippled human life were only the guilt of sin, then the atoning death of the Christ would be a revelation of such love, mercy, and redemptive power that it would wipe away the evil of history. We would be like criminals abandoned to the living death of penal servitude who heard the footsteps of someone bringing a key to release us. Inside our gnarled, brutal bodies, our hearts would melt at the love that sacrificed itself for our wicked, undeserving selves.

But abused children do not need to be forgiven. Kunta Kinte cannot be made whole by having someone else pay a blood offering to remove his "guilt." The sorrow that ravages the innocent, the young, and the persecuted is not relieved by atonement. The suffering even of the Messiah does not remove the stain of this pain. The tiny torture victim in Chile must bear her suffering all on her own; and if she is destroyed by it, she is destroyed—the death of the Messiah could not prevent it.[25]

Nor does the terrible agony on Golgotha make it unimportant that she was destroyed by her tormentors.

The evil that cleaves the fundamental goodness of creation is twofold. First, the sheer fact of suffering and wickedness on this scale and with this intensity is heinous and disgusting. Secondly, this suffering and sinfulness, even the most hideous, is rooted in history prior to any individual action. The disfiguring of freedom by sin and radical suffering is ubiquitous in human history. Not only mortality but susceptibility to *radical* evil are built into the human condition prior to any individual's act or choice, prior to any possibility of guilt.

For creatures who bear the burden and wonder of freedom, radical, destructive evil is the condition of existence. Human beings cannot hope to be free from the threat of radical suffering or to be relieved of the corruptions of sin. It is our doom to live under conditions that destroy us.

But in the midst of history, we can hope for vindication in heaven. "We'll understand it better by and by," as the hymn promises. Eschatology may provide consolation, but it is not redemption. Radical suffering is precisely the experience of hopelessness; it cannot be redeemed by hope. Further, future vindication does not erase the wrongness of being made inhuman by suffering. "Pain cannot be redeemed . . . retribution in the future does not wipe away the pains of the present. There is no justice that could make reparations for it."[26]

If a time comes when every tear is wiped away, when death, mourning, and pain have all ended, there will be release from suffering; but even that cannot make the past as if it had never been. "This recourse to eternity . . . bear[s] witness to the impossible exigency for salvation which must concern the very instant of pain, and not only compensate for it."[27] The world cannot be made whole again, the surd of suffering shatters every attempt to restore harmony. Radical suffering is outside the bounds of justice and cannot be returned to the harmony of justice by consolation, vindication, or retribution. It cannot be *justified.*

> I have no wish to be a part of their eternal harmony. It's not worth one single tear of the martyred little girl who beat her breast with her tiny fist, shedding her innocent tears and praying to "sweet Jesus" to rescue her in the stinking outhouse. . . . No,

I want no part of any harmony; I don't want it, out of love for mankind. I prefer to remain with my unavenged suffering and my unappeased anger—*even if I happen to be wrong.*[28]

No explanation, no act of atonement, no consolation can heal the wound of radical evil. The goodness of creation is *essentially* violated. No terrible sin or ultimate harmony can justify suffering. The pillars of classical theodicies are not available to a tragic vision. The injustice and horror of human anguish compel us to call God to account. In an inversion of the prophet Micah's words (6:1–2), we must cry out to God:

> Arise, plead Your case before the mountains
>   and let the hills hear Your voice.
> Hear, you mountains, the controversy of the people,
>   and you enduring foundations of the earth;
> for the people have a controversy with their God,
>   and we will contend with our Creator.

PART TWO

Toward a Theology of Resistance and Redemption

3

A Phenomenology
of Compassion

*Is not the evil of suffering . . . also the unassumable and thus
the possibility of a half opening, and, more precisely, that wherever a moan, a cry, a groan or a sigh happen there is the original
call for aid, for curative help, for help from the other ego whose
alterity, whose exteriority promises salvation?*
Emmanuel Levinas, *The Provocation of Levinas*

The foregoing chapters describe the problem of evil as one of
tragic fragility and radical brokenness. The radicality of human suffering is such that any *justification* of it must inevitably trivialize evil. There is no theory that might justify
suffering, but there is a labor to resist evil and to heal its destructive effects. The power to resist and redeem evil will not
be like the power that dehumanizes people. Redemption requires liberation and healing; power that dominates, orders, or
manipulates is not the *kind* of power that can free and restore
the human spirit.

Compassion is a mode of relationship and a power that is
wounded by the suffering of others and that is propelled into
action on their behalf. Compassion resists suffering rather
than tries to justify it. It resists suffering by offering whatever
comfort, healing, or empowerment it can within the confines of
a particular situation. An exploration of compassion may provide a way of conceiving of divine redemption not in the eschatological future but now, here, for us, as we encounter the world
in all of its pain, beauty, and cruelty.

The following three chapters attempt to provide an ethical and theological response to evil. The argument will occur in three steps: The first will be a phenomenology of compassion, which temporarily puts aside theological questions. The second step (chapter 4) will appropriate this phenomenology for a theology of divine love. The final step (chapter 5) will relate divine love, especially in the form of compassion, to a history broken by radical suffering.

For the purposes of this argument, compassion is understood to be primarily a power or efficacy rather than an interior emotion. The following phenomenology will look at five aspects of compassion: sympathetic knowledge, disposition, love, justice, and power. Perhaps in exploring these elements of compassion the distinctiveness of redemptive power may begin to emerge.

Sympathetic Knowledge

In order for compassion to respond to suffering, it must have some knowledge of another person's experience. This knowledge must be more than projection or inference if it is to be effective; it must be real *knowledge* of another person's suffering. A commonsense objection to the possibility of such knowledge is that human beings do not have direct access to each other's subjective experience. I cannot rummage around in someone else's experience as I would in a drawer, looking for marbles and matches and old photographs. This objection can be readily granted since obviously I cannot directly experience the pain, grief, or despair of another person.

And yet human beings do in fact talk to each other with some degree of understanding; they comfort, tease, humiliate each other; they learn from or teach one another. All of these experiences presuppose some access to a shared world of meanings, perceptions, values, and feeling.[1] Compassion is a more specific phenomenon than sympathetic knowledge. But it is through this capacity for entering into another's experience that compassion is possible. A brief examination of the general capacity for sympathy may provide a stronger basis on which to understand compassion.

In their writings on sympathetic knowledge, both Edith Stein and Max Scheler distinguish between experiencing an event oneself, in the "first person" (a "primordial" experience), and experiencing it sympathetically.[2] Any conscious experience will be my own, but the content of sympathetic knowledge will be derived from someone else's experience. As an experiencing being I am engaged in the situation, but for the *content* of such an experience (for example, sadness) I turn to the sad person. If I sympathetically share the grief of a friend whose wife has died, the content is the same for both of us, namely, his grief. It differs in that for him it is a primordial experience and for me it is a sympathetic experience. This kind of knowledge of others' experience is contrasted with imitation, projection, or representation. I do not imagine what grief is like, or remember some grief of my own in the past and project it onto his experience. Sympathy enters into another person's experience directly, but nonprimordially. That is, I can *know* that another person is grieving or humiliated or overjoyed, not by inference or projection, but directly. Such knowledge is not, however, immediate experience of the other's grief, humiliation, or joy.

This description attempts to correct two misconceptions. On the one hand, it repudiates the idea that it is either possible or necessary to have primordial experience of someone else's subjective feelings. There is a logical distinction between my deepest and truest sympathy for someone's grief and a primordial experience of grief. On the other hand, it is equally incorrect to suggest that awareness of other people's experience is mere guesswork, the imposition of my own experiences or memories or imaginings onto them. Sympathetic knowledge is authentic, direct apprehension of another's situation that can take me beyond my own autobiographical experiences.

Sympathetic knowledge is an apprehension of a situation or experience precisely *as* belonging to someone else, qualified by the other's interpretation of it, within the perimeters of the other person's own frame of reference. "Can one . . . commiserate more deeply than for his having to suffer as he does, being the sort of man he is?"[3] For example, a friend may have a passion for something you consider idiosyncratic or trivial. Perhaps she has set great store by winning an office talent contest. You may consider the whole affair idiotic. But when the friend loses, sympathetic knowledge enables you to transcend your own opinions and enter into what it would be like *for her* to have lost this thing she wanted so badly. One is not so imprisoned in one's own experience and values that it is impossible to perceive how she feels and to comfort her. Likewise, sympathetic knowledge allows one to rejoice when someone else obtains something one has no personal desire for. A childless career woman who does not want children can feel the happiness of a pregnant friend. Sympathetic knowledge enables one to go beyond the boundaries of one's own desires to experience an event from the perspective of another person.

The distinction between sympathetic and primordial experience should not conceal the relationship that exists between them. Edith Stein argues that primordial and sympathetic knowledge come together in sympathy. She uses the example of sharing the joy of a friend who has just passed her exams. One sympathetically shares the friend's joy and primordially experiences the joyfulness of the event.[4]

Max Scheler, on the other hand, is quite critical of the idea that there is any actual sharing of experiences at a primordial level: "such real suffering does not occur . . . in true fellow-feeling."[5] For Scheler, sympathetic and primordial experience are sharply differentiated; he is suspicious of primordial joy or sorrow, fearing that one is simply savoring one's own emotions. A primordial experience of joy or sorrow is spurious in comparison to sympathy. The moral value of sympathy lies in its power to effect self-transcendence. Sympathy frees human beings from egocentricity, that is, "the illusion of taking one's own environment to be the world itself, i.e., the seeming givenness of this environment as 'the' world."[6] For Scheler, the value of sympathy lies in its power to liberate the ego for the other. Sympathetic knowledge allows one to experience fellow-feeling in a situation where one's *own* feelings may be very different. I can sympathize with my friend who lost the talent contest, even though I thought the contest was stupid in the first place.

It might be added that there could be times when it would be inappropriate for primordial and sympathetic experience to coincide. For example, if a child is afraid of the dark, a loving parent may experience sympathetic knowledge of this fear but not be afraid of the dark himself. Consolation would consist not only in fellow-feeling but in helping the child to overcome her or his fear of the dark. When one cannot or should not feel fear or grief or disappointment oneself, one can feel sorrow in the presence of the other's unhappiness. There usually would be something wrong with a person who knew the pain of another but remained unmoved by it.

Sympathy is real concern for another that frees one from self-absorption and enables one to understand something outside one's own experience. It is a discernment of a reality: namely, another person's experience. As such, it might be likened to the ability of the eyes to see colors or of the mind to grasp the logic of a mathematical proof. Like both of these, it is subject to error.

The capacity for sympathetic knowledge is a condition for compassion. Through sympathetic knowledge, compassion "tastes" the pain, despair, uncertainty, and anguish of the world. Through understanding and fellow-feeling, it enters into others' situations and shares them. Suffering of an intensity or kind that is out of reach of its own primordial experience becomes compassion's own through sympathy.

An Enduring Disposition

Compassion presupposes the capacity to perceive something about another person's suffering, but it is distinguished from sympathetic knowledge in that it is not limited to perception of isolated events. Compassion is a disposition, a way of organizing and interpreting the world that precedes any particular perception or action.[7] Compassion is an *enduring disposition* that functions to integrate the elements of world-engagement. It should not be isolated into a single faculty such as emotion or responsibility. Nor should it be understood as an accidental response to a particular event of suffering. A passing feeling of pity when one hears about some misfortune is not compassion. While it will always be made concrete by particular events and responses, compassion is a persisting way of interpreting and responding to the world.

Human beings are not interior, private Egos or Minds that accidentally begin to relate to a world. A human being *as such* exists in relationship to others, to a society, to nature; consciousness occurs only through participation in the world. Further, a person is not a series of fragmented emotional blips or bits of knowledge juxtaposed like so many incongruous beads on a string. Particular experiences emerge within a cohesive whole. This whole is not a homogeneity but a complexity of

quite diverse elements that are nonetheless integrated together. There is a multilayered quality to consciousness, as if a
chord rather than a single note were being played. Engagement
with the world takes place through a grid of interpretations
and values that occur prior to their expression in particular
feelings or decisions.

Human consciousness consists of many parts: emotion, understanding, cognition, perception, anxiety, desire, social existence, embodiment, and so on. These formal elements of a
person will be made concrete by the primordial disposition
that orients one in the world. Each moment of experience is not
brand new. It is already absorbed into an interpretive grid, a
set of values, and a characteristic way of seeing and responding
to the world. Despair is a disposition: in despair the world is
encountered as hopeless and meaningless. All experiences and
events are seen through the jaundiced eye of despair.

As an enduring disposition, compassion is a qualification of
consciousness that integrates its many dimensions into a cohesive mode of world-engagement. Compassion colors one's consciousness of the world and pulls one into the world in a
distinctive way. An entrepreneur may be directed toward the
world in such a way that relationships, events, and experiences
are grasped primarily through their usefulness or threat to various moneymaking schemes. In contrast, compassion's care for
creatures and for their suffering is the organizing principle of its
experience of the world. While any particular compassionate
person may be limited by blindness or prejudice, compassion
has a universalizing impulse. The whole variety of possible relationships, whether with individuals, with nature, with political
systems or events, will be apprehended through sympathetic
understanding and compassionate responsiveness.

The whole self—as an acting, feeling, understanding, interpreting, valuing, embodied, social being—becomes the servant
of compassion's care for the world. The way one interprets information and ideas, the way one responds to friends or stran-
gers, or the way one understands a political situation will be
informed by sensitivity to other people's suffering.

This is not to say that a compassionate individual is incapable of listening to a piece of music without grieving for hungry
people around the world. Rather, it means that the beauty and
suffering of one's environment constantly impinge upon con-

sciousness and dispose one toward the world in a compassionate way.

An illustration of compassion as an enduring disposition is
found in the vow of the Bodhisattva: "Although sentient beings
are innumerable, I vow to save them all." This vow reflects an
ongoing perceptiveness and commitment to resist suffering in
all its forms: it is a general attitude toward the world that will
find expression in any number of concrete acts and relationships.

Compassion is a characteristic way of interacting with the
world, always expressed in particular acts but preceding them
as a perpetual way of seeing and responding to the world. It is a
disposition rather than a momentary feeling of pity.

A Form of Love

Compassion as response to suffering presupposes knowledge
of suffering. Suffering gives compassion its subject matter, but
it is love that transforms this knowledge into a compassionate
disposition. Compassion is open to the pain of the world because it loves the world. Love gives to compassion eyes to see
the suffering it encounters, and love fires compassion with desire to alleviate suffering. Compassion is the disposition to love
a world filled with suffering.

In English and German "compassion" (Mitleid) means literally "suffering with." This interior connection with another's
suffering distinguishes compassion from externally similar
phenomena such as duty or responsibility. Compassion is similar to duty in that both result in some action on behalf of
someone else. But the pain experienced for the victims of suffering suggests that compassion is closer to love than to moral
obligation.

In order to better place compassion within the general context of love, I will begin by analyzing some general features
characteristic of all love and then discuss compassion as a distinct form of love.

Love itself is such a rich and varied concept that it is somewhat misleading to attempt to reduce it down to essentials.
Love is used to describe an intensity of felt value that may be
fairly superficial (such as "I would love a martini") or even
pathological (for example, the old folk song that goes: "I killed

the only woman I loved because she would not be my bride"). Love that is nothing more than a selfish, if intense, desire for something is distinguished from love that cares for something for itself. It can be generally agreed that what is simply a desire to use or exploit something for one's own ends is at best an ugly distortion of love.

Even putting aside egocentric perversions of love, there remain a number of phenomena that should be classified under the general rubric of love but that are quite distinct from each other. Friendship, *hesed,* charity, romantic love, desire for God, love of nature or art are all distinctive ways of loving. Within this diversity, certain features can be identified that make it appropriate to class all of these relationships as examples of real love. Fundamental aspects of love include: self-transcending delight in something other than oneself, care or concern for the other, and a tendency toward universality.

Self-Transcending Delight

Love is by nature *both* self-transcending and delightful. Its interest and center of gravity lie in the beloved rather than in the self. The essence of love is a liberation from egocentrism that enables one to really care about something other than oneself. Love's freedom from egocentrism allows it to be drawn to what lies outside of itself. Until a relationship is self-transcending, it may be desire or enjoyment, but it is not yet love.

But self-transcendence is not self-abnegation or lofty indifference. Love is delightful. The delight of love is not a sophisticated form of egotism. It means instead that human beings can be really happy caring for and delighting in something other than themselves. There are those theologians who are very concerned to preserve love from any taint of self-interest.[8] The implication is not only that love should be free from egocentrism but that such freedom is necessarily unpleasant.

The ability to enjoy the beauty in the world or the wonderful alterity of another person is possible only through love. Further, liberation from the tedious weight of one's own miserable little ego is not necessarily self-sacrificing but can be profoundly fulfilling. The delight of love is the ability to be enchanted by the loveliness of being. This delight is only possible in conjunction with self-transcendence. Transcendence is not masochistic indifference to oneself but a liberation for the other. It may be considered paradoxical that in love the more completely one forgets oneself, the more contented one can be.

All love entails desire, although of different sorts. Romantic love or the desire for God desires communion and intimacy. Such love hungers for the presence of the beloved and for the mutuality of direct relationship. A nature or art lover desires only to be able to enjoy beauty without interfering with it, possessing it, or changing it. Compassion desires the healing of all forms of suffering but does not necessarily require a personal relationship.

Self-transcendence and desire become two ways of saying the same thing in real love. Love is the capacity to care for and enjoy the other; it is desire that has been freed from egocentricity.

Care

All love is interested and desiring, but its self-transcendence is evident in its ability to expose itself to terrible personal danger when the beloved is threatened. Care and service to the other reflect the dependence of one's own happiness upon the happiness of the beloved. The lover does not look after, protect, or help the other out of duty but because of his or her primordial concern that the other be happy.

Before proceeding, however, I should point out that care for the other's well-being can be imposed as a command and duty, in which case it no longer expresses love. Women in particular have been subjected to a perverse misunderstanding that equates self-immolating service with love. Love is courageous because of its care and delight in the beloved and not out of a self-sacrificing or masochistic indifference to its own welfare. When the robust desire for the other's good is replaced by self-effacing servanthood, it is more likely to be pathology or oppression than love.

Love exists in a tragic world where love and lovers are constantly threatened; care for the beloved is likely to involve danger and effort. The work of the mothers of the "disappeared" on behalf of their children can hardly be described as delightful. But even here where there can be no question of pleasure, love is a blazing fierceness. "Every morning when I wake up, I think only about my sons and about what I can do to take them from where they are. It is as if lions grew inside of me, and I am not afraid."[9] This has nothing in common with pathological self-effacement or with "cool and refrigerating . . . benevolence."[10] It is the fire of love as it confronts evil.

Love is turned toward its object rather than toward itself. If the beloved is in trouble, love is a protecting ferocity. This is not the self-sacrificing martyrdom of love described by Kierkegaard or Reinhold Niebuhr but the natural response of love to danger and evil. In love, enjoyment is no more egocentric than care is self-immolating. Because love presupposes someone to do the loving, it is not and should not be without desire or interest. But because it is a real care for and delight in something else, it is not absorbed in solipsistic pleasure or egocentric fear. In love, self-effacement and egocentricity are equally overcome by self-transcending delight and the courage it lends to the lover.

The Universality and Tragedy of Love

Love enjoys the capacity to recognize and appreciate the loveliness of others. Since everything that exists has its own value and beauty, love has a natural tendency toward universality. There are, of course, relationships that require an intimacy and intensity that cannot be extended to all creatures. But the monogamy of marriage does not prohibit the possibility of loving all things in ways appropriate to them. In fact, there is something pinched and narrow in love confined to only one object.

Love is both intensive and extensive. By its nature, it is endowed with a capacity to appreciate the particular beauty and distinctiveness of a great variety of beings. But love exists in a world in which creatures and ecosystems are threatened, not only by evil or mortality, but by each other. Conflict is an inevitable part of the world. Love is in the peculiar position of loving the tiger feeding its crying young as much as it loves the bereaved mother of a young gazelle. It must love the murderer as well as the victim and his family. More terribly, in responding to conflict and violence, it may be in the position of having to inflict suffering when its natural desire is to protect and delight in all creatures.

Love cares for all creatures, but suffering and conflict are inherent in existence. It is the tragedy of love that it cannot rest in the simple delight in all creatures but must see them suffer and engage in the work to help them. Because of this shadow side to love, compassion must be its constant companion. Through compassion, love enters back into a situation that is broken by suffering and evil, not simply to suffer with the beloved, but to redeem it.

Compassion and Love

Compassion is love as it encounters suffering. But given the ubiquity of suffering, the love of creatures will always be tinged with compassion. Compassion shares the general features of love, including its care for and delight in others. Compassion combines knowledge of the dignity and value of creatures with sympathetic knowledge of suffering. But compassion is primordially a power; its knowledge of creatures and their suffering serves as an entree through which to mediate the power of love.

Pity is sometimes used as a rough synonym for compassion. But pity lacks compassion's respect for the sufferer. Pity is usually a lack of respect for those in trouble, "an insult, a backhanded thrust at self-respect, the unkindest cut of all."[11] Condescending pity is a common enough phenomenon, but it is antithetical to compassion. Compassion is sympathetic knowledge of suffering that mediates dignity to the sufferer. To receive compassion is to receive respect.[12]

Compassion as a form of love includes a recognition of the value and beauty of others. Far from insulting the sufferer with gratuitous pity, it mediates to the other a sense of her own integrity. It sees through the suffering and recognizes the goodness that is not destroyed by the suffering; this recognition of the personhood of the sufferer allows compassion to sympathize with her. This in itself is comforting. Compassion identifies suffering as an affront to this integrity, as an anomaly that threatens and defaces the sufferer; it identifies the wretchedness of her situation as alien to her.[13]

Victor Hugo describes the mediation of respect to Jean Valjean, an ex-convict. Such respect is a hallmark of the effect of compassion. Jean Valjean finds his way to the home of the local priest, Bienvenue, who puts out the good silver and brings up the old wine for this stranger:

> Every time he [the priest] said this word "monsieur," with his
> gently solemn, and heartily hospitable voice, the man's counte-
> nance lighted up. *Monsieur* to a convict is a glass of water to a
> man dying of thirst at sea. Ignominy thirsts for respect.[14]

Suffering defaces the natural beauty of a creature; compassion restores self-respect and so counters this effect of suffering. But there are sufferings that are necessary to heal a
disorder; this is especially clear in the case of wrongdoing or
medical treatment. Compassion will not censure such suffering
but will sorrow for the necessity of it. Compassion will not
abandon sufferers to their suffering, even if it is necessary or
deserved. Even pain and guilt cannot completely efface the dignity of the human being in compassion's eyes. Compassion
mediates a sense of the contingency of the suffering and the
absoluteness of the dignity and in this way becomes an agency
to resist the dehumanizing effects of suffering. Even if the suffering itself cannot be avoided, it can be endured and used for
ultimately healing purposes.[15] In the absence of compassionate
presence, necessary suffering can be dehumanizing rather than
restoring.

The relationship between Sonia and Raskolnikov in *Crime
and Punishment* portrays compassion as the power that enables punishment to be ultimately redemptive. Raskolnikov
murdered two of Sonia's friends. The saintly Sonia is appalled
when he confesses to her but is even more overwhelmed by his
diseased suffering. " 'There is no-one in the whole world now
so unhappy as you!' she cried in a frenzy. . . . A feeling long
unfamiliar to him flooded his heart and softened it at once. He
did not struggle against it. Two tears started into his eyes and
hung on his lashes."[16] But for all her compassion, Sonia insisted Raskolnikov turn himself in to the police. She never
approved of his action or tempted him to avoid punishment.
Instead, she agreed to accompany him to Siberia. In this way
she enabled him to finally experience redemption and freedom
from both his guilt and the sickness that occasioned it.

Sufferers are tortured when deprived of the last vestige of
self-respect by the "back-handed insult" of pity, but they long
for the consolation of real understanding. Compassion is able
to provide this understanding through sympathetic knowledge
of suffering. Compassion enters into the situation of anguish
and shares it. If suffering finds consolation in understanding,

it is not because it is wallowing in self-pity or because it sadistically wants the other also to suffer. Suffering isolates its victim, so that alienation intensifies the experience of suffering. Solidarity and real understanding can ameliorate feelings of isolation that accompany suffering. Compassion does not stand outside the suffering in handwringing sympathy. It does not peer down on the victim and demand a stoicism that denies the pain. It begins where the sufferer is, in the grief, the shame, the hopelessness. It sees the despair as the most real thing. Compassion is with the sufferer, turned toward or submerged in her experience, seeing it with her eyes. This communion with the sufferer in her pain, *as she experiences it,* is the presence of love that is a balm to the wounded spirit. This relationship of shared, sympathetic suffering mediates consolation and respect that can empower the sufferer to bear the pain, to resist the humiliation, to overcome the guilt.

Sympathetic knowledge enables compassion to participate in suffering, mediating courage and love to the sufferer. In a primordial experience of suffering, pain and humiliation can efface the dignity of the suffering. As sympathetic experience, compassion participates in the reality of the suffering; but the primordial experience of compassion is love. It can remain unscathed by the destructive effects of suffering. A primordial experience of love combines with a sympathetic experience of suffering to resist the overwhelming effects of suffering and to mediate this power of resistance to the sufferer.

There is a distinction between sympathetic and primordial suffering that is not the coolness of indifference. It is a distance through which compassion is present to suffering with the intimacy of sympathetic knowledge but with a power that brings light to dark places. The playfulness of love faces evil and suffering and finds it can do so, and do so with redemptive power, through compassion.

Justice

Compassion is an enduring disposition of love that resists suffering. It empowers life by opposing what degrades it and therefore finds justice to be a constant traveling companion.

Justice entails principles of equity, of fairness. For example, justice is the "maintenance of positive legal order . . .

[through] the distribution of riches, power, and honor according to just deserts, . . . [and punishment of] every violation of the positive legal order."[17] Justice has to do with providing a system for distributing the goods and burdens of a society and for addressing violations of this system.

Compassion corrects the incipient legalism or callousness of blind justice. It provides justice with a hatred of suffering and a love for all creatures, without which justice can become demonic. "Justice dies when dehumanized, no matter how exactly it may be exercised. Justice dies when deified, for beyond all justice is God's compassion. The logic of justice may seem impersonal, yet the concern for justice is an act of love."[18] Justice and compassion complement one another both in discerning what a just distribution might be and in determining how to address violations of a system of justice. The relationship between justice and compassion in these two domains, social injustice and wrongdoing, will be investigated in turn.

Social Injustice

In contrast to the principles of distributing riches, power, and honor according to some criterion of merit, the Hebrew prophets seemed to understand justice as a positive condition for human fellowship. "Justice may be properly described as 'the active process of remedying or preventing what should arouse the sense of injustice.' What is uppermost in the prophets' mind is . . . the presence of oppression and corruption. The urgency of justice was an urgency of aiding and saving the victims of oppression."[19] This is a sensitivity which is quite different from that contained in the foregoing description of distributive justice. Justice is a vision that arises from the anger and sorrow over suffering caused by oppression. Justice is no longer "an exact proportion of duties and rights"[20] but a recognition of human dignity and a struggle to maintain conditions of fellowship.

The desire for justice in this sense, like compassion, arises from an intuition of the unassailable dignity of human beings. Policies or institutions that erode or ignore this dignity are understood by the Hebrew prophets to be scandals before God. Hunger, racism, and brutality violate human beings; they are outrageous and perverse. Justice is the restoration of the positive conditions of human dignity. It is the acknowledgment of the claims of human beings to whatever is necessary to secure their existence. All things "call on us with small or loud voices. They want us to listen, they want us to understand their intrinsic claims. . . . This of course is also the source of all injustice. If the new decisions destroy the essential claim of a being, they are unjust."[21]

Justice overarches legal right and condemns a legality that would undermine fellowship or that fails to listen to the intrinsic claim to dignity and well-being that all human beings possess. The prophets do not recognize the right of the wealthy to amass property at the expense of the poor (Isa. 5:8–10; Amos 5:11). Injustice is not problematic as a violation of law but as a violation of others. Its consequences are not legal transgressions but chaos and wanton violence that disrupt personal and social relationships. "When Cain murdered his brother Abel, the words denouncing his crime did not proclaim: 'You have broken the law.' Instead we read: 'And . . . the Lord said: what have you done? The voice of your brother's blood is crying to Me from the ground.' "[22]

Justice is more than legalism, but it is through legal and social systems that societies are organized, either to secure conditions of equity or to codify exclusions and oppressions. The power of institutions, governments, and laws to oppress and destroy makes social justice a necessary expression of compassion. Because so much suffering and destruction are the effects of political and social policies, compassion engages in political activity. This labor will become concrete in any of the endless ways in which people struggle against human degradation, but no matter what form it takes, compassion includes the work of justice in the political arena.

Wrongdoing

To some contemporary Christians, the relationship between compassion and justice is an obvious and straightforward syllogism: injustice causes suffering, compassion acts to overcome suffering, therefore the struggle for justice is an inherent activity of compassion. This is, as we have seen, true. Compassion is naturally expressed in the work to alleviate suffering caused by oppression.

Compassion also is present in the justice that calls evildoers to account. Abraham Heschel warns against sentimental indifference to cruelty, describing unconditional forgiveness as a Pandora's box, "a fine incentive to vice. Anger is a reminder that man is in need of forgiveness, and that forgiveness may not be taken for granted."[23]

A conflict arises in compassion between its striving against the causes of suffering, which include cruelty, injustice, and evil, and its striving for universality. This conflict creates a tension in compassion, but it can be a creative rather than a tragic tension. Compassion surpasses the narrow ethics of retribution and legalism by striving simultaneously against cruelty and for every creature. It is precisely this two-edged concern that radicalizes the ethics of compassion so that it becomes authentically redemptive.

Compassion's sense of justice is based on its recognition of human dignity. This dignity is not destroyed by wrongdoing. Compassion condemns acts of violence or cruelty but is incapable of objectifying a person as guilty. Further, the brokenness and anguish of sin evoke compassion. The Buddha saw humankind drowning, "their hatred condemning them to endless retribution. For all of this Buddha was moved to pity."[24] Compassion extends to stupidity, to violence, to the diseased spirit that enjoys cruelty, and to the retribution that violence brings to itself. "As I live, says the Lord GOD, I have no pleasure in the death of the wicked, but that the wicked turn from his way and live; turn back, turn back from your evil ways; for why will you die, O house of Israel?" (Ezek. 33:11).

All forms of brokenness call forth compassion, even the bentness of sin. There is an abandon that is proper to compassion. It is limited only by the limits of human brokenness and yearns for all types of healing. The stories of Jesus' ministry suggest this abandon in compassion. He is portrayed as associating with outcasts and madmen, Roman legionnaires, tax collectors and prostitutes. His healing hand is remembered as extended to the excluded, poor, and sick, and to the sinful as well. He defends his ministry to society's morally handicapped by pointing out that "those who are well have no need of a physician, but those who are sick; I have not come to call the righteous, but sinners to repentance" (Luke 5:31–32). Pity for suffering and help for the righteous might be expected of any decent person. But the radicality of compassion is shown in the labor to redeem sinners and to liberate human beings from their own evil.

Just as compassion criticizes a legalistic understanding of justice by insisting on a positive vision of social equity and harmony, compassion also criticizes a legalism that contents itself with punishing the wicked. In both cases, it extends justice to include a positive restoration of well-being. Compassion challenges the axiom of moral thought that retribution is the only adequate response to guilt. It undermines the logic of punishment with the logic of redemption. It does not sacrifice condemnation of wrongdoing but seeks to overcome it rather than simply punish it.

Compassion is unlike law because it is intoxicated by love for all creatures. For it, the first work of justice, even in relation to wrongdoing and guilt, is to preserve human dignity. Punishment that is dehumanizing cannot be redemptive and is therefore not justifiable. Compassion cleaves the logic of punishment with the logic of grace and mercy. In this way guilt is not balanced with an infliction of suffering but is overcome.

We live in a world where crime and violence are part of the status quo. Criminals and governments alike use terror, torture, and brutality to maintain power. It is wrong not to demand that these people be held responsible for their crimes. The question is how they will be held responsible. Compassion, whose other face is justice, insists that responsibility be meted out with eyes on the humanity and dignity of the wrongdoers as well as on the violations they have committed.

The Reverend Dean Tshenuweni Simon Farisani, a victim of torture in South Africa, talked with Americans who had worked for his release from prison. They wished him well in his continuing human rights work. He replied: "And pray also for those who took me, since when I go to heaven they also must come along."[25] Farisani thus pierces the *jus talionis* with the radical vision of compassion. Creation is a tragic, beautiful web; it will discover justice only when the twistedness of sin and the brokenness of suffering are healed together.

Power

Compassion describes a distinctive way of engaging the world that has an efficacy for transformation. In it, sympathetic knowledge of suffering becomes a kind of power. Compassion represents a fundamental alternative to the power of domination or coercion. It contends for sufferers, not like a white knight—steel on steel—but as a different *kind* of power.

Power, Not Domination

Jean Baker Miller argues that the meaning of power, as it reposed in the hands of those who intended to maintain dominance, "acquired overtones of tyranny." For women, power means rather overcoming past marginalization: specifically, it means the "capacity to implement."[26] Untainted by the desire to dominate, power means simply the ability to act or to effect something in the world.

The meaning of power is often derived from those who most obviously have the force to effect their will: kings, tyrants, and executioners. Power almost comes to be identified with force and its means: domination, violence, and manipulation. The fulfillment of such power is destruction; it kills or destroys whatever thwarts it. The sheer force of sovereignty is worshiped, even as it inspires terror.

Compassion stands in opposition to this construal of the nature of power. Compassion is not helpless before force, as impotent kindness; but neither does it accept force's definition of power. Process thought attempts to describe power that is not simply force, distinguishing the power of coercion from that of persuasion. Process thought represents a great advance on this front but does not go far enough. Persuasion is a benign authority, but it is still authority, though it is unclear in what sense it is efficacious. This distinction between coercion and persuasion avoids the idolatry of sheer force, but it does little to suggest the sense in which love might constitute a distinct *kind* of power.

Empowering Power

Compassion mediates the courage to resist suffering. One of the most destructive elements of suffering is that it causes self-respect to deteriorate. A sense of fatalism, of deserving to suffer, of hopeless ennui helps to chain victims to that which assaults them. Suffering becomes self-perpetuating and absolute. In order to confront external conditions of injustice and pain, the power to resist must be mediated to the victims of suffering. If compassion only worked externally, it would fail to affect this fundamental level of suffering, which is the destruction of freedom and self-respect. If it were lordly and magnificent, giving people what they need, it would be charity that tacitly perpetuated the conditions of suffering. Compassion is a power that gives people their own power; in this way it overcomes the dependence and despair that are among the most debilitating effects of suffering.

Shelters for battered women provide an example. These women have two problems: one is the immediate physical threat of their husbands, the second is their psychological and economic dependence on these men. Shelters provide a sanctuary, temporarily addressing the first problem. They also provide the means for women to begin making themselves independent without going out and solving their problems for them. Shelters provide protection and advice to battered women and mediate the courage and self-respect women will need to find ways of helping themselves.

Compassion labors to make whole human beings out of broken ones. But it must do this in ways that acknowledge human beings as free, as creatures of spirit. Sin and radical suffering dehumanize individuals and communities so that they are incapable of resisting the evil in their midst. Effective resistance includes the courage to resist the destruction of the spirit as well as the situation generating the suffering. Resistance to these kinds of brokenness requires an internal power; compassion, in opposing them, must be an empowering agent.

Gustavo Gutiérrez distinguishes authentic liberation from policies of development. Development is designed and implemented in ways to protect and even entrench economic and political structures that result in poverty and that maintain patterns of dependence. Gutiérrez writes: "Poor countries competed for the help of the rich countries. . . . But since the supporters of development did not attack the roots of the evil, they failed and caused instead confusion and frustration."[27] Under the auspices of a plan to help a country to develop itself, patterns of domination and dependence were instead deepened. In contrast to the paradigm of development, Gutiérrez argues that only when the poor are empowered to participate in economic and political structures for themselves will authentic liberation occur. Likewise, the role of compassion is not primarily to do things for others but to empower those who suffer to speak and act in their own defense.

External aid, food for the hungry, jobs for the homeless, medicine for the sick are sacraments of compassion's care. But compassion goes further and attempts to empower human beings to resist injustice and to fight despair and guilt themselves. The Buddhist parable of the mustard seed tells of a woman who is driven almost mad by sorrow when her infant son dies. She is sent to the Buddha for help. The Buddha "seeing that she was ripe for conversion," sends her on an errand that will help her to discover *for herself* a way out of despair. "Full of compassion for the welfare of mankind," the Buddha does not interfere or even give her any direct advice or consolation. He guides her on the path that helps her to obtain for herself freedom from suffering.[28] Compassion repudiates the magnificence of charity in order to heal the indignity of powerlessness and dependence perpetrated against the human spirit.

I have used the example of Jean Valjean from *Les Misérables* to illustrate the dignity that compassion gives to sufferers. But compassion not only dignifies the humiliated, it effects the power of redemption. In Victor Hugo's novel, the encounter with a radical and unconditional compassion serves as the agent of Jean Valjean's redemption. Jean Valjean steals from the priest who had been so kind to him. When he is arrested and returned to the priest for identification, Bienvenue insists that he *gave* the silver to Jean Valjean, and even gives him his last two candlesticks. The act is one of radical and gratuitous compassion. Jean Valjean has been so embittered by his years of prison that he seemed beyond redemption. But the shock of this utterly unjustified, spontaneous compassion so resonates in his soul that he finds healing and redemption. The priest's compassion recognizes and responds to his dignity and sorrow. This recognition touches him in his inmost self and mediates a healing power. The fatal wound begins to heal, the hood of despair and cruelty that covered his mind is removed; he again feels hope and the vitality to lift himself from the depravity into which he had sunk.

The power of compassion is such that it cannot be absolute. The efficacy of redemptive power is not a natural force like gravity that exercises causal necessity upon its object. It does not gain possession of a creature and subject it to its will, as might the torturer, or doctor, or judge. Compassion is an offer, a presence: it requires mutuality and relationship and therefore is contingent upon response. For Jean Valjean, compassion served as a condition for his redemption, but it could not exercise causal necessity. The compassion of the priest had to be complemented by his own struggles and responses. It would have been possible for Jean Valjean to be glad to "get off the hook," without experiencing the *metanoia,* the liberation from his bitterness and hatred. Compassion is a condition for redemption but does not possess mechanical compulsion; it mediates healing power but does not determine a response.

Les Misérables portrays the redemptive power of compassion as it affects an individual. But the arena of compassion's labor is not limited to the inner healing of broken individuals; it is a comprehensive way of existing in and toward the world. Compassion is a mode of world-engagement. It is a pattern and power in history that resists the power to hurt, maim, and dehumanize.

Power for Domination

J. R. R. Tolkien's *The Lord of the Rings* depicts an epic struggle between good and evil. As such, it is similar to most other fantasy novels. It differs from other fantasy literature in that it portrays this struggle as between two fundamentally different *kinds* of powers. For Tolkien, the struggle between good and evil is not like that between Beowulf and Grendel; it is not a contest of strength.

In Tolkien's story, evil is concentrated in the Dark Lord, in Sauron, who is, at the opening of the adventure, beginning his final gambit to gain control over all of Middle Earth. Sauron, in an earlier age, made a ring of power. He poured all of his power into this ring. With it, victory would be assured. Unhappily for him, the ring was stolen from him and has been lost for many centuries. Before his mastery can be secured, he must find this ring.

Tolkien's understanding of the nature of evil becomes clear

in his description of the ring of power. The ring itself is a plain gold band. It is a beautiful thing. It grants power to its wearer according to the kind of strength he or she already has: a warrior will become bolder, a wise person more clever, etc. But it corrupts its possessor with a desire for possession. Not only does the ring grant dominion and strength, it exerts an irresistible temptation to *desire* domination. It is never inert or neutral; it cannot be used against Sauron. To use it at all will make one a victim of its lust for possession and control. Even if Sauron were defeated, the new owner would be compelled to place herself or himself on Sauron's throne, becoming a new Dark Lord. Regardless of how pure one's original motives, the use of the ring for good would inevitably corrupt one so thoroughly that one would become its vassal. It is the nature of evil that it exercises an *irresistible* temptation to dominate.

The power characteristic of evil is domination, violence, and terror. The force of evil is stronger than good, but it relies on terror as much as on sheer strength to overcome opposition. The power of Sauron's nine henchmen resides more in the terror they inspire than in their actual physical strength. Sauron has a kind of military genius, but neither terror nor military might is the quintessential expression of his power. The most terrible dynamic of evil is that it corrupts the good. All of Sauron's tools threaten to tempt, beguile, and enslave those who resist him. Saruman, the leader of the Council of the Wise, and the good steward Denethor both find themselves seduced and then destroyed when they enter too closely into Sauron's mind in their attempts to spy out his ways. Evil can trap and destroy its opponents using their own desire for good as bait.

Compassion seems to be the power that holds out longest against evil. The hobbit Frodo is terrified to learn that the pretty little gold ring he inherited from his uncle Bilbo is in fact the terrible ring of power. He suggests that it was a pity that Bilbo did not murder Gollum, a miserable creature from whom he accidentally obtained the ring. Gandalf replies: "Pity? It was Pity that stayed his hand. Pity, and Mercy: not to strike without need. And he has been well rewarded, Frodo. Be sure that he took so little hurt from the evil, and escaped it in the end, because he began his ownership of the Ring so. With Pity."[29]

Power for Preservation

The power characteristic of the good is quite different from that of evil. It is the power of creativity, wisdom, and compassion. Three rings made by the elves demonstrate the distinctiveness of what is good. "They were not made as weapons of war or conquest: that is not their power. Those who made them did not desire strength or domination or hoarded wealth, but understanding, making, and healing, to preserve all things unstained."[30] The sylvan paradise of the elves, Lothlorian, and Rivendale, the home of Elrond the Wise, are both created and preserved by elven rings of power.

Real power is resident in what is good, but it is a power alien to the desire for strength or domination. The struggle between Sauron and the denizens of Middle Earth is not symmetrical. For the "free peoples" there is no hope that they can win a war against Sauron, he is too strong; battle can at best distract him from his real threat. If Middle Earth is to protect itself against Sauron, it cannot be through warfare. The asymmetry between good and evil is evident partly in evil's vastly superior strength; it is irresistible while the good is always subject to corruption. The asymmetry is also seen in the blindness of evil. Sauron's mind is open to Galadriel, the elven queen, though hers is not open to Sauron. He is blinded by the assumption that he will be resisted on his own terms: in a battle for domination. Sauron cannot imagine that anyone would not want domination; it is inconceivable to him that anyone would want to *destroy* the ring of power. Notwithstanding his superior strength, he lacks the wisdom and insight to be indomitable.

Middle Earth cannot resist Sauron with weapons of war, with terror of their own, with corruption, threat, or domination. Their only hope is to destroy the fountainhead of evil: the ring, which gives Sauron his power and which corrupts all else with the desire for dominion. They must take the ring into the land of shadow, into Sauron's stronghold, and destroy it—a mission so hazardous and ridiculous as to be the sheerest folly.

> "Despair or folly?" said Gandalf. "It is not despair, for despair is only for those who see the end beyond all doubt. We do not. It is wisdom to recognize necessity, when all other courses have been weighed, though as folly it may appear to those who cling to false hope. Well, let folly be our cloak, a veil before the eyes of the

Enemy! For he is very wise, and weighs all things to a nicety in the scales of his malice. But the only measure that he knows is desire, desire for power; and so he judges all hearts. Into his heart the thought will not enter that any will refuse it, that having the Ring we may seek to destroy it. If we seek this, we will put him out of his reckoning."[31]

The power of what is good is absurdity before the sheer might of Sauron. And yet this foolishness is their only hope.

Although in Tolkien's story Sauron is defeated, victory was not without its price: the defeat of Sauron brought in its wake the destruction of things that could not be rebuilt and the loss of a beauty that could never be regained. Frodo's maiming, in body and soul, is a microcosm for the fate of Middle Earth. It was freed from the threat of utter destruction, a new age dawned, but the struggle against Sauron diminished Middle Earth in ways that could never be healed. In the struggle against evil, good will be maimed even if it is not destroyed.

Tolkien depicts two world orders. Evil is stronger and it is irresistible. Evil corrupts desire. It is the strength of dominion and the desire for possession. This order cannot be resisted on its own terms. One must repudiate the desire for domination: this in itself is the heart of the struggle against evil. It is the genius of J. R. R. Tolkien to see that the difference between good and evil is one of opposing types of desire and power; whenever good is tainted by the desire for dominion and control it has already lost the battle and been overcome by evil.

"Contact with the sword causes the same defilement, whether it be through the handle or through the point."[32] The very existence of evil is destructive, even if it is not ultimately victorious. Evil bites deeply into the world; its potency for destruction is not simply an external conflict consummated in military battle. The world is wounded by *the very need to resist evil;* the power of evil is such that it always inflicts a wound, even if it fails to completely destroy its victim. There is a tragic dimension even to victory, which is distinct from destruction, but distinct from triumph as well.

The Folly of Compassion

It is the nature of evil to subvert even the struggle against evil. One way the struggle against good is enervated is by juxtaposing power and goodness. Resistance to evil is replaced by complete passivity. This dualism between murderous power and passive victimization absolutizes domination and deprives victims even of the dignity of resistance.

A second way to subvert resistance to evil is the temptation to use force and violence for some good end. There are benevolent and malevolent uses of force: if force is used for a good end, murder and domination are supposedly cleansed of their wickedness.

In theologies stressing the divine sovereignty, God is portrayed as omnipotent and more or less benevolent. But the *type* of power represented by domination is intrinsically corrupt. Any power that is causally absolute, even if motivated by a good will, necessarily deprives other creatures of any real activity, participation, or uniqueness. There can be no benevolent but absolute power, because such power by its very nature deprives creatures of the possibility of freedom.[33] Omnipotent sovereignty is not the power of a love that values creatures; it is the benevolence of a slave owner, who is "kind" to slaves but still deprives them of dignity and responsibility. The relationship between master and slave, between the powerful and the powerless, cannot be cleansed of its degrading effects.

The power to dominate cannot be cured of tyranny, but neither can redemption be accomplished passively. It is not necessary for compassion to resign itself to benign handwringing because power is corrupt and oppressive. Neither is it necessary for compassion to appropriate patterns of domination or force in order for it to be efficacious. The alleviation of suffering cannot be accomplished by external manipulation; domination requires a servile will as its counterpart. Compassion is power to bring to life what is broken by pain, to bring to justice and redemption what is twisted by brutality, to free creatures from the torment of self-absorption and enliven them for care and delight and creativity.

Power as domination or even as benevolent coercion cannot redeem because it falsifies the nature of human being and it betrays the nature of love. To resist suffering demands strength and courage, hence power. This is the internal paradox of compassion: it is a power but it cannot coerce. It must rest in this uneasy tension, empowering others to resist suffering without becoming indifferent or overwhelming.

Redemptive power gives power to someone else: it is empowering rather than controlling. The failure of compassion need not be traced to its impotence but to its relational character. A creature broken by pain or twisted by wickedness may not have the courage or desire or energy to respond to compassion, and compassion cannot take the citadel of suffering and sin by force. "O Jerusalem, Jerusalem, killing the prophets and stoning those who are sent to you! How often would I have gathered your children together as a hen gathers her brood under her wings, and you would not!" (Luke 13:34).

Compassion can be frustrated by the recalcitrance of sin and the hopelessness of suffering. But it remains untempted by the seductions of dominating power. Compassion repudiates the methods of force and coercion and wears the disguise of weakness; this is its folly. But this is folly that respects the uniqueness and beauty of every creature and opens a space for each one to delight and work and create for itself and in community with others. It is through the disguise of weakness that compassion gives to creatures their own strength.

Force and domination are temptations to the desire for the good: they appear to be direct and easy ways of overcoming resistance, struggling against evil, saving those who suffer. But, like Sauron's ring, they corrupt whatever they touch. Compassion is the folly of weakness. This entails real folly because it bears enormous risk. Force and terror can and do win victories, every day, every hour. Compassion is fool enough to engage in the serious, destructive struggle against the stronger power of evil.

4

A Phenomenology
of Divine Love

*For as truly as there is in God a quality of pity and compassion,
so truly is there in God a quality of thirst and longing. . . . And
this quality of longing and thirst comes from God's everlasting
goodness, just as the quality of pity comes from his everlasting
goodness.*

Julian of Norwich, *Showings*

Theodicy begins as a complaint against God; the horror and
injustice of suffering compel people of faith to call God to account. How is it possible to worship a God who brings into
being a world such as this? Notwithstanding the damning evidence against God, I will try to show that divine love is deeper
even than the evil that tears creation, and that God is neither
indifferent nor powerless before evil.

Love has been a central symbol for the reality of God in the
Christian tradition, but it has tended to have little influence
on theodicies. More typically, the issue of divine sovereignty
lies at the heart of discussions of evil. If God is omnipotent, it
is necessary to trace evil and suffering to God. Theodicy attempts to justify God's decision to permit, tolerate, or make
use of evil in creation.

The difficulty with posing the problem this way is that it
juxtaposes love and power as two alien entities. Omnipotence
is the absolute power to control and dominate creation. Love is
primarily mercy. The divine sovereign chooses to redeem some
of those who actually deserve punishment. The sacrificial

death of the Logos of God dramatically reveals this choice to redeem sinners. But even agapaic love does not affect the sort of power attributed to God. Redemptive love alludes to a particular way of using omnipotent power. In the drama of salvation, love is restricted to the role of motivating omnipotent power: it does not make any real impact on the *meaning* of power.

A second reason divine love tends not to play a very central role in Christian theodicies is that theologians have been uncomfortable about directly attributing love to God. At most it expresses human experience of divine actions. Love and mercy are attributed to God metaphorically "as seen in its effect, but not as an affection or passion. . . . To sorrow, therefore, over the misery of others belongs not to God; but it does most properly belong to Him to dispel that misery."[1]

Theology's hesitation to attribute love to God derives in part from its profound sense of the transcendence of God; no quality or experience or concept can be attributed univocally to God. There is a certain sentimentality (at best) and idolatry (at worst) in *equating* any human experience or construct with divine being. Also, although Christianity tends toward anthropomorphic and relational metaphors for God, theology resists the temptation to imagine God as a cosmic person. God is not *literally* a heavenly father complete with emotions, prejudices, and preferences. Love is an intimately human experience; it infringes on the mystery and transcendence of God. The abysmal alterity of God cannot be confined by any concept, including that of love.

Yet human beings continue to struggle toward some way of relating the empirical ubiquity of unjust suffering to an intuition of ultimate goodness. Faith and theology seek some language that would aid them in making sense out of evil. Evil and God are poles of a mystery that remains impenetrable to symbols and concepts. But the experiences of suffering and of faith yearn for expression in language. Theology is, at best, an uneasy truce between the radical mystery of God and the limitations and idolatries of human language.

Christian theologians have shown a certain wisdom in their circumspection. Love is hopelessly anthropomorphic and emotional. Theology quickly degenerates into banality and sentimentality when human emotions are attributed to the transcendent mystery of ultimate reality. But as a symbol of divine power, love has certain advantages over sovereignty or *actus purus*. It represents a fundamentally different *kind* of power than the power of coercion.

The phenomenon of radical suffering becomes both more sensible and more bearable if it is conceived of in relationship to divine love. Love is not a power that is causally absolute: if the power of God is conceived of through the grid of love rather than sovereignty, there is "room" in creation for that which utterly resists and thwarts the will of God. Evil need not be attributed to God, as punishment, purgation, indifference, or testing. It need not be incorporated into a vision of harmony, which somehow *needs* the torment of children or the eternal punishment of sinners to perfect creation. Evil is instead that which has successfully resisted God. It is a surd, an anomaly. The risk or foolishness of divine love is that it creates a world in which real and terrible resistance to God is possible.

Imagining divine power through the symbol of love makes it possible to account for evil without having to *justify* it. It also illuminates the power of God to resist evil. The afflicted are not beyond the pale of God's power but at its very heart. The cross symbolizes this struggle of God for the world, not externally, not in judgment upon it, but in the very midst of the most radical anguish and evil.

Love provides an alternative paradigm to that of sovereignty and domination. In this way, a space is opened to reflect on the unjustifiable character of radical suffering. A tragic vision is concerned with resistance to evil rather than justification of evil. Creative and redemptive power is interpreted through the paradigm of divine love. In relationship to evil, divine power is that which makes resistance to evil possible; it is not modeled after power that dominates and destroys. Compassion, as a determinate form of love, symbolizes the struggle to transcend and redeem evil.

I will suggest reasons why love may be a helpful paradigm and then analyze four dimensions of divine love: ungroundedness, eros, tragedy, and compassion. I am using love as a root symbol to express the goodness and power of God; by uniting images of goodness and power in a single symbol, the tension between them may be overcome.

Love as a Paradigm of Divine Power

As a noncoercive form of power, love creates the possibility of evil by leaving freedom and the future undetermined. The consequence of the nonabsolute character of love is a tragic context to freedom. Love also symbolizes power to oppose evil. It correlates to that element of tragic vision which seeks to transcend tragedy. Reasons for the appropriateness of love as an expression of divine power can be found both within the logic of a tragic vision and within the logic of redemption.

The Tragic Vision

The ancient Greek tragedians portrayed the dynamic of tragic suffering against a background of conflict or malevolence. Something in the hero's environment fated her or him to destruction. Zeus *(Prometheus Bound)* or the Fates *(Oresteia)* or a curse *(Oedipus Tyrannus)* provides the tragic context of the hero's actions. Tragic heroes are defeated by forces beyond their control, and this seems to suggest that the world order itself is evil. But every tragedy also is transcended; a vision of justice or vindication qualifies the injustice described by the play. It is as if two opposing world orders struggle against one another in the background of the plot: one testifying to the injustice of the cosmos, the other to an ultimate good that lies deeper than the destruction of the tragic hero.

When power is no longer construed according to a pattern of domination, both of these world orders might be traced to a single source: the tragic structure of divine love. It is the genius of divine love to permit authentic alterity: "the great force of the idea of creation . . . is that this creation is *ex nihilo* . . . because the separated and created being is therefore not simply issued forth from the father, but is absolutely other than him."[2] Not only is finitude ontologically other than divine being, but human freedom is also other than the divine will. Both ontologically and morally, the creative power of divine love is manifest in that which is radically other than God. Love is a *kenosis* of the plenitude of power. It is realized, not in pure unity and self-sufficiency, but as the power to generate the strange wonder of difference.

But the alterity of creation is simultaneously its fragility.

Creation is other than God and so vulnerable in ways that divine being is not. Conflict among values, creatures, ecosystems, religions, and nations is the permanent environment of human action. Intellectual, moral, spiritual, and physical fragility confine human freedom. This tragic environment to existence is the shadow side of finitude. What is expressed symbolically in Greek tragedies as the inevitability of conflict, and by malevolent deities, is an environment shattered by conflict and preexisting evil. But from the perspective of a Christian tragic vision, the harsh environment to freedom need not be traced to a wicked cosmos. Instead, it appears as the tragic structure of divine love. The power of love brings alterity into existence, but the fragility of alterity is intrinsic to finitude and cannot be overcome.

Divine love as the source of a tragic world order is also the source of the vision of justice, vindication, and compassion that transcends tragedy. The destruction of what is good, the diminishment of hope, the triumphs of force and brutality are all too real. But destruction is not the only reality. There remains a freshness that is undefiled, a resistance that is not entirely battered down. The ultimate vindication of Antigone, the Voice that speaks to Job from the whirlwind, do not undo the violence and injustice that has occurred. But they testify to some other reality than that of absurdity and suffering. These twins, tragedy and resistance to tragedy, are born together: the harvest of divine love as it comes to expression in the alterity of finitude.

Redemption

Conflict and evil in history reflect the tragic structure of divine power. But this power, as the power of love, is also expressed as redemptive power. The interior reality of divine being remains hidden: it is the unnameable "cause of *being* to all; but itself: non-being"; and it defies all attempts to delimit or describe its power or reality.[3] But the abyss between God and the world is thinly bridged by divine causality. For religious consciousness, "God" names that power which is the foundation, not only of existence, but of liberation, enlightenment, and healing. In its relationship to the world, God is known as redemptive power. "We have the sense of divine love directly in the consciousness of redemption, and as this is the basis on which all the rest of our God-consciousness is built up, it of course represents to us the essence of God."[4] Whatever God may be in Godself, *for us,* the power of God is essentially the power of redemption. The power and will to redeem are more aptly symbolized by love than by models of domination, judgment, or control.

It is arguable that compassion and love provide the most characteristic ways in which the Hebrew and Christian scriptures understand divine being. God is first known to Moses as One who says: "I have seen the affliction of my people who are in Egypt and have heard their cry because of their taskmasters; I know their sufferings, and I have come down to deliver them out of the hand of the Egyptians" (Exod. 3:7-8). Even after Israel's betrayal of God in the incident of the golden calf, God's self-revelation to Moses is as "a God merciful and gracious, slow to anger, and abounding in steadfast love and faithfulness, keeping steadfast love for thousands, forgiving iniquity and transgression and sin" (Exod. 34:6-7).

Redemption—from slavery in Egypt, from exile in Babylon, from persecution by the Greeks and then the Romans, from sickness, sin, and death—is one of the foundational experiences through which the biblical writers interpreted divine power. Love and compassion express the power of God as a *redemptive* power.

For Christians, divine power is most clearly and poignantly seen in the Messiah, whose teachings, death, and resurrection manifest the love of God "made flesh" in history. I cannot turn aside at this point and enter into the murky regions of Christology. However, the stories of the Christ seem to illuminate God's relationship to the world as essentially redemptive. In contrast to the cosmic indifference of Aristotle's Unmoved Mover and to the strict, mechanical justice of the Fates, God is revealed through Jesus Christ to be a power of redemption. In the Synoptic Gospels, Jesus is portrayed as struggling against the evil of the demonic world, evil as the suffering caused by exclusion, poverty, and hunger, and against evil in the form of sin and guilt. All forms of evil that disrupt life are contested by the Messiah. The radicality of love is evident in its extension to all those who are excluded—either by society (women, lepers, the insane) or by their own guilt (tax collectors, prostitutes, Romans). In the paradigmatic events of the Bible—the exodus or the coming of the Messiah—the power of God is manifested as the struggle against evil and as liberation from historical and spiritual oppression.

A central metaphor of redeemed existence is communion, especially as table fellowship. Healed relationship is the sign of redemption. The strangeness of the biblical conceptions of God is that they suggest that the infinite power of the divine has something at stake in the world. Love symbolizes not only the power of God against evil but also this striving for communion, for relationship. Redemption consists not only in forgiving or healing isolated souls but in bringing them into relationship with one another and with God.

Love expresses the distinctive *kind* of power that is not coercive but healing. It attests to the relational character of redemptive power. The value of alterity; the priority of relationship over isolation; compassion in the face of suffering; the repudiation of domination, terror, and judgment are contained in the symbol of love. Like all other language about God, it cannot be understood to coincide with divine being. It can degenerate into sentimentality or idolatry. But the logic of tragedy and redemption warrants its appropriateness as a point of departure to aid reflection on the relationship between God and suffering.

Ungroundedness

Thomas Aquinas begins his reflections on the divine attributes by stating that "we cannot know what God is, but rather what he is not."[5] This reticence is necessary to preserve the sense of mystery that veils the sacred. The metaphor of ungroundedness qualifies a phenomenology of love by evoking the ineffable abyss of divinity. It functions both to preserve the mystery of God and to symbolize the vital depths of the divine life. Jacob Boehme, the Lutheran mystic, uses the metaphor of the *Ungrund,* ungroundedness, to describe the first moment of the Godhead. It is a metaphor corresponding to the first person of the Trinity or to Hegel's moment of unity that precedes separation and reconciliation. It is an attempt to express the "godliness" of God, the utter mystery and transcendence of divine being:

> When I consider what God is, then I say, He is the One; in
> reference to the creature, as an eternal Nothing; he hath neither
> foundation, beginning, nor abode; he possesseth nothing, save
> only himself; he is the will of the abyss; he is in himself only one;
> he needeth neither space, nor place; he begetteth himself in him-
> self, from eternity to eternity.[6]

Ungroundedness is a metaphor for the mystery of God. It is a
reminder that negations lie before and after the symbols or
concepts for ultimate reality: God is not anything in the world
nor is God *like* any aspect of finite being. Finitude is contingent and finds the reason or power of its existence outside of
itself. But God is "ungrounded": no external ground or power
gives being to ultimate reality. This is the most basic difference between God and creation: the difference between contingent existence and aseity.

Human beings have some intuition of the reality of God
through the experience of redemption. But the being or reality
of God is hardly exhausted by this experience. Without this
first principle of divinity, language about God quickly disinte-
grates into a moral ideal or metaphysical principle. The word
"God" becomes little more than the projection of our desires,
values, or fears. Appeal to "God" becomes the warrant for our
political adventures or religious ambitions. A culture's principles of sexual morality become identified with the divine will.
"God" evokes a clean, secure feeling or disgust at such archaic
superstitions. In these ways transcendent reality is emptied of
its holiness.

Tillich describes this first principle as the intensity of divine
being; it represents the fundamental abyss that lies between
creation and God, and likewise, between human concepts and
divine being.

> The first principle is the basis of Godhead, that which makes
> God God. It is the root of his majesty, the unapproachable inten-
> sity of his being, the inexhaustible ground of being in which
> everything has its origin. It is the power of being infinitely resist-
> ing nonbeing, giving the power of being to everything that is.[7]

Tillich apparently did not sense the irony of describing
that which transcends all human concepts in masculine
terms. His own description of the radical transcendence of
God implies that gender-specific language for God is ludi-

crous and even idolatrous. The symbol of ungroundedness qualifies the sense in which it is possible to speak analogically of human and divine love. Divine love is not only free from the various limitations of human love, it is immersed in this "unapproachable intensity" of being that qualitatively transforms love. Ungroundedness qualifies theological claims as the principle of negation, but more precisely as the principle of divinity. Ungroundedness represents the inadequacy of human thinking to divine being. God utterly transcends the categories of finitude: being and nonbeing, change and changelessness, time and timelessness. Ungroundedness is the infinity of divine power; it is a metaphor for the incomprehensible grandeur of God.

That which grounds finitude while transcending its distinctions is the nothingness of divinity. It qualifies language about God, responding to every affirmation with a negation. But this groundless abyss is the source of love as well as of mystery. "The divine life is infinite mystery, but it is not infinite emptiness. It is the ground of all abundance, and it is abundant itself."[8] Ungroundedness qualifies a phenomenology of divine love as a symbol for the holiness or transcendence of God.

Eros

The first principle of divinity is ungrounded infinity. *That* God is not reducible to our concepts and experiences is as much as can be positively said about God's own being.

Love is a symbol for the relationship between God and the world. It is rooted in human experiences and ideas and therefore reveals more about how Christians conceive of God than about God's own being. But it may be hoped that the symbol of love, in expressing something about human experience, may illuminate something about God as cause of the experience of redemption.

In the previous chapter, I argued that self-transcending delight was one of the essential characteristics of love. Love is directed toward the other in care for and delight in its existence. Further, relationship is an essential quality of human existence: we do not live as isolated monads but in personal, political, and ecological relationship with one another. Love is the fulfillment of relationship. It enables one to recognize and respond to the value of all creatures. Love is the perfection of a system in which creatures exist in relationship and, ideally, in relationships of love and care.

A phenomenology of human love does not directly, univocally apply to God but must be strained through the ungrounded reality of divine being. The classical theological tradition has refrained from attributing to God human emotions: anger, mercy, love, desire may have some metaphorical value in describing the *effects* of divine power in history, but they say nothing whatsoever about the divine life. This puts a seemingly arid and abstract deity in the place of the deeply passionate God of the Bible. But it also disciplines theology, reminding it of the ultimate mystery of God.

Eros is not intended to describe the emotional life of divine being but rather to symbolize an aspect of divine power. Desire expresses the insufficiency of self-sufficiency. Eros is a symbol for the transition from self-contained unity to creative power.

Christian theology has, with some notable exceptions, refused to attribute desire to God. Desire implies lack and therefore imperfection. That which is already and eternally perfect cannot need anything. There remains, unfortunately, the annoying facticity of creation.

Thomas Aquinas accounts for desireless creativity by way of a Platonic metaphysics. Being itself is perfectly good; one of the features of the good is that it communicates itself.[9] Divine being is like the sun; it is perfectly self-sufficient but sheds its enlivening rays abroad on all things. Eternal self-contemplation is the fullest expression of perfection, but it has as a side effect, so to speak, the gratuitous communication of existence to finitude. Beings exist because they participate, however inferiorly, in the perfection of divine being. God does not need or desire or enjoy creation. The attribution of need, desire, or enjoyment to God undermines the fulfillment of divine self-contemplation. God creates by self-communication —but without desire, says Aquinas.

Self-communicating, desireless perfection protects divine being from emotional or ontological entanglements with creation. It preserves the majesty and integrity of transcendent divinity. I, for one, hesitate to undermine the profound sense of transcendence and graciousness conveyed by this metaphysical description of God's creative powers.

And yet, the implication of this metaphysics is that self-enclosed identity is the ideal of perfection. Difference and relationship diminish perfection; they are anomalies. The goodness of ultimate reality is thus set in direct opposition to the perfection of creation. The perfection of human existence occurs through the harmony *achieved* by love; the perfection of infinite being is a self-contained, even indifferent, unity. Naturally, one cannot expect finite goodness to correspond exactly to the perfection of God. But one might expect an analogy of goodness between God and the world. A radical disjunction between the perfection of God and the striving for perfection in human beings would suggest that God could not be the power of redemption. If God is its cause, redemption should in some sense reflect the causal efficacy of divine power. If this power is essentially one of interior self-contemplation, then the effect of redemption would be isolated monads rather than a community of love. If there is no causal or analogical connection between divine power and the effects of redemption, then nothing is left to connect human beings to ultimate reality. But if God is causally connected to human beings as the power of creation and redemption, and if both creation and redemption are constituted by relationships, then a relational symbol for divine perfection may be more appropriate. Eros symbolizes the greater perfection of relationship over self-contained unity.

Desire as a symbol of divine creativity does not express lack or imperfection. It is rather the perfection of relationship. "The true desire . . . is goodness. . . . It is the lack in a being which *is* completely, and lacks nothing. Can the Platonic myth of love, son of abundance and of poverty, be interpreted as bearing witness to . . . the insufficiency of what is self-sufficient? Has not Plato, in the *Symposium* . . . affirmed the non-nostalgic nature of desire, the plenitude and joy of the being who experiences it?"[10]

The metaphor of divine desire challenges the philosophical priority of unity. Desire describes a dynamic process that moves from unity to self-expression or creativity. It is constituted by a dialectical balance and tension, a harmony of parts. The logic of love replaces a paradigm of undifferentiated unity with relationship and motion.[11]

The first moment of perfect unity in which lies the grandeur and majesty of God comes into relationship with finitude through the act of creation. Jacob Boehme uses the metaphor of hunger to describe the *telos* toward self-expression in the divine. "For nothing hungereth after something, and the hunger is the desire, viz. the first Verbum Fiat, or creating power."[12] The attribution of time or development to God would, of course, undermine the principle of negation that governs theological discourse. The point is not that, in some literal sense, there are stages or moments of the divine life. Rather, the metaphor of desire or hunger illustrates the inadequacy of unity as an expression of the relationship between God and the world.

Desire symbolizes the *ecstatic* character of divine creativity. The perfection of divine power stands outside of the interior, unknown life of God and is manifest in creation. The barren plenitude of self-contemplation erupts in the power of creativity. The dynamic of creation is the exteriority of divine power: finite existence intimates that divine power is not self-contained and is not exhausted by self-contemplation but rather finds expression in creation. Erotic power tears away at nothingness and brings into existence that which is radically other than itself. Creation is a footprint of the power of God to resist nothingness. It is a sign that the perfection of God includes ecstatic creativity as well as contemplation. "The divine life is creative, actualizing itself in inexhaustible abundance. The divine life and the divine creativity are not different. God is creative because he is God."[13]

The power of God is known to human beings—however faintly and ambiguously—through its effects. Creation is a sign of the value of alterity. This value is symbolized by the divine eros, whose needless and eternally perfect reality externalizes itself in creation.

Tragic Love

An internally tragic structure to the power of love and to finitude thwarts divine creativity. Desire symbolizes the manifestation of divine power in creation. But, as I suggested in chapter one, finitude is fragile in ways that make conflict, suffering, and distortion inevitable. Divine love is universal, but particular creatures are in conflict. Creative power empowers the tiger to feed its hungry young, as well as the gazelle that tries to flee the tiger.

Although individual creatures cause suffering—microbes infect mammals, predators destroy their prey, religions persecute one another—God must share responsibility for suffering. Creative power culminates in a world in which conflict and evil are not merely possible but inevitable. Divine love cares for creatures who must suffer; the power of tragic love is displayed in the nurture of a cosmos in which conflict is unavoidable. Human beings care for the beloved in situations that exist over against human well-being. The defenders of the Warsaw ghetto in World War II resisted a situation that assaulted them from outside. But divine love is tragic in the more profound sense that it addresses suffering within a context that it created itself. A theology of divine love finds itself in a similar position to theologies of sovereignty: both in the end must attribute the existence of evil to God. But for a theology of love, evil occurs as the inevitable consequence of finite existence. Fragility and conflict cannot be exorcised from creation but must coexist with the wonder and beauty of nature as the price finitude pays for existence. The desire to lavish life and love on alterity is thwarted by the very conditions of finitude. The exuberance of eros becomes the deadly serious labor of tragic love to ameliorate the evil occasioned by *its own* creative act.

Compassion symbolizes the power that resists the destructive effects of sin and radical suffering. But suffering and evil that do not destroy and rupture human existence also occur. The book of Job does not depict God's compassionate power to redeem Job but places his suffering within the context of a complex order of nature. Appeal to the vast mystery and beauty of nature is presented as evidence that suffering does not itself indict God as an evil or unjust being. Tragic love for creation underlies God's response to Job. God resists and limits the forces of chaos but acknowledges conflict and suffering as inevitable counterparts to the diversity of creation. Divine wisdom orders nature so that all creatures are valued while destructive possibilities are restricted, but God still feels the sting of Job's accusations and feels compelled to respond to them.

The book of Job is the story of a righteous man who suffers unjustly. Accepting the commonly held view that the universe is constructed according to the laws of distributive justice, Job is distressed that he, a righteous man, should suffer. Job's anguish is not reducible to his losses or even to his own physical affliction. His life is unbearable because he has lost the order and meaning his faith gave to his life. His faithful redeemer has become his enemy and persecutor. A just world order has given way to absurd and meaningless suffering. Since Job is certain of his innocence, suffering can be evidence of nothing other than divine treachery. Job loses patience and calls God to account for God's betrayal; he demands a hearing, a court appearance, to clear his name. Clinging to the hope that God is good and just, he tries to believe that his persecution was due to some celestial clerical error. But there was no error. The problem becomes one of clearing not Job's name but rather God's own name.

The divine defense consists in a description of nature. God unfolds before Job's eyes the structures of the world, evoking the wildness, beauty, and paradox of creation. God describes the beginning of creation, "when the morning stars sang together, and all the sons of God shouted for joy" (38:7). At the beginning there is celebration and joy as well as mirth. The destructive forces of chaos are as harmless as a baby in diapers (38:9).

There is a lot of frolicking in God's creation, the stars sing, the ostrich and horse laugh, the wild beasts play. There is a tender love for mothers and their young. The value and needs of each are respected—the lion's need for prey, the importance of a safe birth to mountain goats and hinds, the desire of the young to go out on their own. The deserts and wastelands must be watered even where no creature lives, for the sake of the grass. Even the fierce behemoth and leviathan are part of the vigor of creation.

God tacitly acknowledges that Job's suffering has no moral justification, but is unwilling to accept the inference that God must be wicked: "Will you even put me in the wrong? Will you condemn me that you may be justified?" (40:8). Yet the Voice makes no attempt to *justify* Job's suffering through theories of retribution, purgation, chastisement, or heavenly compensation. Job's suffering must remain cruel and hard, unjustified, pointless. But the absence of any justification of suffering is not a condemnation of God; it is rather a reinterpretation of how God is related to the world.

Law reduces all experience, whether of fortune or suffering, to an explicit intervention of God. Job's "comforters" seem to imagine that God stands in constant judgment of the world, tinkering with it so that good is rewarded, evil punished. But the Voice suggests a somewhat different mode of presence. Norman C. Habel argues that the book of Job is an attack on mechanistic, legalistic theodicies. *Job* points to "the aesthetic, the playful and comic in Yahweh's design. . . . Both the majestic and the absurd seem to celebrate this design; and Yahweh seems to rejoice in his paradoxical creations."[14] Job's suffering is not ended by the explanation from the whirlwind, but even so, Job takes back his accusations and leaves his ashheap.[15] Job is restored to God because he understands that suffering does not make God his enemy. Job comes to realize that worship of God occurs not with the hope or even desire for rewards but as an end in itself; reconciliation is the wisdom to see that suffering does not negate the goodness of God or the value of life.

The book of Job addresses the problem of evil from the perspective of the conflict and struggles inherent in nature. Suffering is part of existence, but it does not testify to the indifference or malevolence of God. Divine power is extended to every creature as the power of existence. Divine love and pity are evident in the story of Job in God's delight and care for all creatures, in God's tenderness for mothers and their young, and in God's willingness to respond to Job. Most of God's defense consists in describing God's providential care of nature as having independent value and needs from human beings. This is not an anthropocentric vision of the world. God makes fun of the idea that human beings could tame the wild ox or ass or defeat the huge behemoth. God protects these creatures from servitude and destruction. God causes it to rain in places where no human being will ever dwell. Suffering and even unjust suffering are placed within the broader context of a world that is not limited to human wants or needs. Conflict and suffering are unfortunate side effects of an enormously rich, humorous, and paradoxical creation.

God is not a careful judge, weighing our sin and rendering punishment; this is not God's role or God's way. As Whitehead says, there is a touch of amorality in love.[16] Strict justice would condemn what kills, but God cannot help loving the golden beauty of the lion as well as the leaping joy of leviathan. God permits a great deal of diversity in creation, loving it all. It is not that God is indifferent to Job's suffering; the point is that it is impossible to eradicate suffering from creation. Variety cannot be tamed without negating the possibility of existence. The structure of life is not law but wisdom and celebration— and tragedy.

But the wisdom to discern the goodness of God in the midst of inevitable suffering is insufficient to the radical suffering of history. The rupture of creation through sin and radical suffering calls for a redemption that goes beyond tragic love.

Compassion

Creation is bent by suffering, broken by evil. It requires not only wisdom but redemption. Compassion symbolizes the power that struggles to go beyond tragic wisdom to authentic healing. Divine love is manifest to creation as compassion— not to suffer with creation but to redeem it.

The argument developed in chapters one and two is that evil comes about not through the sovereignty, powerlessness, or indifference of God, but through the tragic structures of finitude and freedom. Human beings can suffer, and they can be cruel. In giving history authentic autonomy, the creative power of God is paradigmatically revealed. But autonomy is also separation from God that prevents history from perfecting its freedom. The divine eros has a tragic destiny in history: it desires relationship and shuns possession or manipulation. Love is fulfilled in mutuality that is both an overcoming of separation and the preservation of autonomy. Creative power preserves alterity through reciprocal love. But humanity remains separated from God and incapable of returning divine love.

In the relationship between God and history two levels of separation exist. The first exists between God and all autonomous beings as that distance both created and overcome by eros. Separation or difference is the condition for relationship. Love requires an other. The second level is the separation effected by sin and suffering. These evils rupture the fragile continuity between God and creation; an abyss of pain and cruelty hides God from history so that separation becomes isolation. The savagery of history is testimony to this long defeat of God by humanity.

The power of love expressed in creation (eros) and in providence (tragic love) is complemented by the power of redemption. Compassion is divine power in a new guise, the guise of redemption. As history is ruptured by the radicality of evil, the power of love is intensified to become the more radical power that resists evil and restores what is broken. Compassion serves as a paradigm through which it is possible to understand how God is related to a world torn by evil. Compassion is a perennial structure of redemptive power. It symbolizes the enduring presence of divine love in the world as an interactive, reciprocal power. Compassion is attentive to the concreteness of suffering and sorrow; it is active in ways appropriate to the particularities of a given situation. As a symbol of divine power, compassion is not a mechanism through which God is related to history—like the Torah, the church, or the atoning death of the Messiah. It is a description of the sort of power that is present in redemption.

The ungrounded transcendence of God qualifies the symbol of compassion, as it does all symbols and concepts of the divine. Because divine love emerges from this abyss, it cannot be understood to be identical to the human phenomenon of compassion. God may be known as the eternal "Thou," but God is not a person. Human compassion is a mode of world-engagement that presupposes embodied, historical, psychological, anxious, social, and political existence. It is characterized by the presence of one physical, linguistic person to another, or as actions of individuals and groups as they intervene on behalf of other creatures. It is mediated by the touch of a hand, the look in someone's eyes, by physical intervention (yanking the child out of the burning house), and by political actions. Obviously, divine compassion will not be like any of these forms of presence or intervention. The phenomenology of compassion that preceded this chapter will serve as a guide to uncover the sort of thing compassion is, but it cannot be uncritically or directly transferred to God.

Compassion offers the possibility of transcending tragedy because it is *resistance* to evil. Eros is the power of God to bring being from nothingness; tragic love is providential care for a cosmos immersed in inevitable suffering and conflict. Compassion immerses itself in evil in order to struggle against it. The primary difference between tragic and compassionate love is that compassion transforms the knowledge and sorrow of suffering into a fierce power of resistance. Tragic love cares for the world, but it is compassion that mediates redemptive power. Redemptive love presupposes sympathetic knowledge of suffering. But in compassion this sympathetic participation in suffering is accompanied by *power* that struggles to transform evil into a locus of healing. God "knows" the sufferings of the Hebrew slaves. This knowledge is not solidarity that "suffers with" the slaves. It is translated into action: "I have come down to deliver them out of the hand of the Egyptians" (Exod. 3:8). According to Christian theology, God's knowledge of suffering is radicalized in the incarnation. The immediacy of knowledge of suffering and evil is here again, accompanied by transforming power. The utter desolation and helplessness of crucifixion is, for Christians, the ultimate revelation and enactment of God's power to redeem human beings.

Compassion does not refer to an emotion or attitude but to an efficacy. The compassionate God is therefore to be distinguished from the benevolent but impotent deity who "suffers with" the world. Redemption requires not only solidarity with suffering but opposition to its destructive effects. Compassion is the intensity of divine being as it enters into suffering, guilt, and evil to mediate the power to overcome them. As human beings and communities apprehend the presence of divine compassion for them and with them, they experience power to resist the degrading effects of suffering, to defy structures and policies that institutionalize injustice, and to confront their own guilt. Compassion as a form of love is mutual and interactive; as a power for redemption it entails the acknowledgment of freedom. The power of love bears no resemblance to a benevolent tyrant manipulating history or to a cosmic magician who will fix our problems. A compassionate human being will sometimes intervene on behalf of others, but the compassion of God empowers. Divine compassion is not a form of paternalistic charity but a more radical love that offers liberating power.

Compassion symbolizes the characteristic mode of relationship between God and evil. But as interactive power, it cannot determine a response to it: it can offer, but it must also be accepted. It can also be refused. Resistance to God can create a "famine of the word"; evil can "eclipse" God from history, but compassion remains available, even if our ears become deaf and our eyes blind to it.

For Christians, the symbols and stories of Jesus, through which the early church tried to interpret its experiences of redemption, provide clues for understanding how divine compassion is present to history. One of the more striking features of many of the Christian scriptures is the radical sense of divine presence experienced by the fledgling Christian communities. This sense of divine presence was mediated in a particularly raw and immediate way through the person of Jesus. This experience of presence gave rise to a variety of attempts to express the meaning and identity of Jesus. The "incarnation" of God in the Messiah symbolizes the intensity of redemptive power available through the life and death of Jesus of Nazareth.

Incarnation as a symbol of redemptive power in history is a compelling paradigm for divine presence. The Christian scriptures do not limit this sense of presence to the person of Jesus (although in later times, "incarnation" did take on more technical, Christological connotations). Incarnation alludes not only to a temporary historical aberration but to a characteristic way in which God is present and active in the world. The parable of the sheep and the goats in Matthew 25 depicts the presence of God, not as a supernatural power to manipulate events, but in the poor, the sick, the hungry, and the sinful. "As you did it to one of the least of these my brethren, you did it *to me*" (Matt. 25:40). The resurrection appearance on the road to Emmaus, which concludes the Gospel of Luke, portrays redemptive presence experienced through sharing a meal together. Table fellowship makes God present among human beings. The Johannine Gospel and epistles associate knowledge of God with obedience to the love commandment. It is in love and fellowship that redemptive power is made present to the community. "Abiding" in God's love is the medium of incarnation, first in Jesus, but continuing in the community. Through mutual love, the incarnation of God in Christ remains manifest and active in the church. God is "seen" in Jesus because of the intensity of love between them. Jesus encourages the community gathered in his name to continue to make God present in the world through their love for one another. It is these acts of love and compassion that continue to incarnate God in history.

> For Christ plays in ten thousand places,
> Lovely in limbs, and lovely in eyes not his
> To the Father through the features of men's faces.[17]

The incarnation of God in Christ, in the poor, in a community, symbolizes the efficacy of divine power in historical existence. The possibility of experiencing divine redemption through a person or historical event testifies to the self-revealing, self-manifesting nature of God and to the potential openness of creation to its creative ground. Incarnation speaks of an event or person that has become sufficiently open to the power of God that, in a more or less fragmentary way, divine power becomes manifest in it. This incarnation of God in and for the world is a breathtaking and radical element of the "good news." History itself—mundane, boring, ambiguous, exciting, and evil history—is the place where God is present with redemptive power.

The continuing incarnation of God in history imbues all action with the possibilities of redemptive power. Care for nature, the desire for justice, the struggle for peace, affection for one another are all sacraments of God's living presence in the world. Through interhuman compassion and justice, the reality and power of God are present to resist evil in history. This potential intensity of divine presence has as its danger the potential for error and forgetfulness of the ambiguity of incarnation. But history remains open to the redemptive power of God through the perennial incarnation of this power.

Through compassion, creative love is augmented by the labor to restore what has been assaulted by evil and guilt. It is a work whose genius and glory are to give life and freedom to creatures who have already betrayed and been betrayed by these gifts. Humanity is broken by bondage to the evils of sin and suffering. Compassion as empowering presence is the sublime and holy power of mercy, comfort, justice, and redemption.

The concluding chapter of this work will apply this analysis of divine love to the problem of evil, proposing ways to interpret the presence of divine power in the midst of tragedy and evil.

5

Divine Compassion
and the Problem of Evil

Mine, O thou lord of life, send my roots rain.
                Gerard Manley Hopkins, "Thou Art Indeed Just"

Compassion is the incarnation of divine love as redemptive power against the domination of evil. It is directed against the tyranny of suffering and sin to redeem humanity not *from* their historical, natural existence but *for* responsibility and joy within this existence. I will first describe divine compassion in relationship to suffering, then to sin, and finally I will discuss the power of divine compassion in history to resist and redeem evil.

Compassion and Suffering

Divine compassion symbolizes the power of God present within the essential hopelessness of history. Eschatological symbols of heaven or hell, of a New Jerusalem, or of the lion and lamb lying down together, are expressions of this hopelessness. Eschatology is hope that must be projected onto a transhistorical future because there is so little hope for history. But if redemption is limited to hope for future consolation, then divine power is removed from creation. Redemptive power should not be understood as alien to history and limited to a transhistorical hope. The immediacy of hunger, of sorrow, of anguish; the wickedness of injustice; and the viciousness of violence demand an immediate response. Compassion resists all suffering and injustice because the poignancy of pain is too unbearable to await future vindication.

But if the power of compassion is not confined to eschatological consummation, neither does it rely on the hope that every pain, every injustice, every hard-heartedness will be eradicated. Compassionate power is the enduring struggle against historical evil. Divine compassion is not mercy to sinners at the end of time but the fight for life during all time. All forms of suffering evoke compassion: the contingency of natural disaster as much as the contingency of human wickedness calls forth divine compassion. But the power of compassion is not to be conceived as a hand coming from the sky to stop the lava flow from destroying the village or to snatch the young girl out of the hands of the rapist. The way in which compassion responds to suffering should not be construed on the model of physical intervention. The power of compassion is incarnational, interactive. It is present to sufferers as the power to resist their suffering in whatever ways are possible within the confines of a particular situation. Compassion cannot magically alter the course of geological history in order to save a village from a natural disaster; such a response to suffering and its causes is not contained within the parameters of the event. Compassion is a power to redeem from suffering, but one made determinate by the specific possibilities contained in any actual situation.

Any event of suffering can serve as a veil, concealing the ultimacy of goodness behind the finality of pain. In radical suffering, this power dominates, but all suffering threatens to overwhelm sufferers in this way. This power of suffering to absolutize itself, as well as the intrinsic sorrowfulness of suffering, calls forth the need for redemption. Compassion therefore takes two courses. The first is to resist the causes of suffering. The second is to resist the power of suffering to dominate sufferers. Divine compassion is directed toward the restoration of wholeness and freedom in all aspects of creation, eschewing dualisms between spirit and body or redemption and politics.

Compassion is evoked by a concrete event or situation of suffering and is responsive to the possibilities of redemption available within it. Suffering caused by systems of injustice and suffering caused by acts of violence are examples of a kind of affliction that can, in principle, be resisted. In such cases, compassion works to empower a community or an individual to resist the violation to which it is subject. The civil rights movement in this country serves as an example. Through a constellation of historical events, the cruelty of American apartheid was confronted and resisted. From the heart of the black community, the courage to face beatings, murders, rapes, imprisonment, and terror was combined with a prophetic vision of justice. Racism was condemned by resistance to the suffering and injustice it caused; in this way compassion gave rise to a vision of equality and to the courage to labor for it.

This example illuminates a kind of suffering that can be resisted and indicates that a compassionate response to it lies in condemnation and resistance, not merely in consolation. Compassion condemns what causes suffering by inspiring and enabling effective resistance to it.

Compassion also directs itself against inevitable or hopeless suffering by resisting the power of suffering over the victim. *Not all suffering can be effectively resisted,* and much suffering that can be resisted is overcome only after a long and terrible struggle that leaves many dead and destroyed before the victory is won. Compassion is present not only in the form of justice but also as consolation and courage. If a human rights worker is cruelly tortured, whether the cause is won or lost, the suffering creates an immediate problem. This is equally true of a person who faces starvation or death in the electric chair or the agony of a horrible disease. Sufferings, for a cause or for no cause, as an individual or as part of a group, occur that have no resolution and offer no hope of escape. In the midst of hopeless or intolerable suffering, redemption cannot lie only in the expectation that the suffering will cease. It will lie instead in the capacity of the sufferer to still taste the presence of divine love even through the torment. In the midst of suffering, redemptive power is present to prevent it from stealing a final victory. Even in hopelessness there is resistance to the destructive power of suffering.

Here again it is the work of compassion to empower sufferers; this time not for the work of change but to break the dominion of suffering over the spirit. Compassion labors to penetrate the darkness of pain and mediate to the sufferer the taste of love and the power of courage. In the deepest pit of

suffering, divine compassion is present to bring comfort and
light, to nourish the spirit battered by pain or humiliation. The
death of the Messiah on a cross testifies to the incarnation of
compassion even in the midst of the most horrible evil. When
freed from theologies of penalty and substitution, the symbol
of the cross reveals the historical struggle of divine love against
the assaults of sin and suffering. This terrible death manifests
the divine presence as the power of redemption in the midst of
history, in the midst of concrete suffering, rather than as effect-
ing a satisfaction of divine judgment.

The debilitating effects of suffering do not occur only in the
more dramatic examples of death camps, torture chambers, or
famine-stricken countries. People whose external situations
are characterized by comfort and security can also be destroyed
by suffering. A woman trapped in a loveless marriage or a creative person trapped in a miserable, routine job can also find
their lives sapped and destroyed by the enduring defeat of despair. The Willy Lomans of the world *(Death of a Salesman)*
cry out for redemption as passionately as do victims of persecution. That is, the redemptive power of compassion is not
limited only to those sufferings to which Christians are especially sensitive at a given time in history. *All* forms of suffering
and destruction are included within the scope of compassionate power.

God labors in every situation to mediate the power of compassion to suffering. That is why it is possible that people can
experience the vilest and most cruel assaults and through
them discover a deeper sense of divine love and a courage that
they themselves mediate to the world. "Neither death, nor life,
. . . nor anything else in all creation will be able to separate us
from the love of God" (Rom. 8:38–39) because divine compassion is directed toward every event of pain and suffering. God is
present as the power for redemption in every situation, but
suffering can bite so deeply that it is impossible for people to
feel its presence.

One of the most terrible beliefs of Christianity is that God
punishes us with suffering. It is a belief inflicted on grief-
stricken or pain-ridden individuals to justify their suffering
and on groups to justify their continued oppression. The association of suffering with punishment denies even the right to
resist suffering. The sufferings, exclusions, and violence caused

by patriarchy, for example, are justified as just punishment for Eve's disobedience or for the alleged moral inferiority of women. The right to transform a situation of oppression is denied. Further, this sadistic theology conspires with pain to lock God away from the sufferer, for whom God becomes the ostensibly righteous torturer. The love of God is gone, and the pious sufferer is betrayed into the hands of despair. This is the theology of Job's "comforters," who heap despair onto suffering by trying to show that God, too, has turned against the sufferer.

God is infinitely compassionate and tender toward the world. Suffering comes because our bodies are frail and because human beings can be cruel to one another—individually and through institutional structures. God labors night and day, like a mother comforting a delirious child, to soothe the fever, to penetrate the suffering and despair. Nothing separates God from the world, but suffering can be a veil that hides this loving presence. In the midst of suffering, compassion labors to tear the veil.

Compassion and Sin

Sin is a form of brokenness, an assault on and corruption of the spirit. It is different from suffering in that it entails wickedness. Sin is a complex phenomenon: it is communal as well as individual; it is bondage as well as guilt; it is the source of injustice and of many cruelties but it is also that which incapacitates human beings for experiences of joy and fulfillment. It is often the case that people observe the phenomenon of sin and see only the simplicity of guilt. The logic of retribution appears compelling and absolute.

Compassion is extended even to moral evil. While cruelty evokes anger, the complexity of sin means that anger is not the final word. To the eyes of redemption, sin and suffering must be overcome together. The web that holds them together, and that holds together all of reality, cannot be divided into pieces without destroying the whole.

In the face of sin, compassion becomes determinate as mercy. This is the annoying and insulting thing about compassion: it seems to be too softhearted; it will not take guilt seriously and make itself hard so it can deal with it appropriately. Forgiveness is a virtue, of course, but there are limits; there are times when it becomes a vice. It is disgusting to think of forgiving the murderers at Auschwitz or Bergen-Belsen.

Classical Protestantism took sin with the utmost seriousness but needed to leave room for the gracious mercy of God. Typically, this was done through the doctrine of double predestination. On the one hand, a few vile and worthless sinners are snuck into heaven, hiding in the white robes of Christ. On the other hand, other sinners, no better or worse than the first, are condemned to unending torture in hell. In the persons of the elect, divine mercy is revealed; in the persons of the damned, divine justice is manifest.This heaven/hell bifurcation confuses mercy with a *reductio ad absurdum* of retribution. The forensic categories of reward and punishment remain intact but are rendered absurd since they are based on fiat rather than merit. Divine mercy is not an absurd application of law but a complete alternative to legal categories. Divine mercy replaces the logic of retribution with the logic of redemption. Mercy permits outrage over wickedness to be accompanied by redemption from sin.

To the ethical mind, good is rewarded (or let alone) and evil is punished. This is so clear, so obvious and straightforward, that it becomes the cornerstone of ethical and religious thinking. Evil cannot be wished away by well-meaning, if vacuous, blindness to its destructiveness. If mercy is not an absurd application of law, neither is it an amorality indifferent to brutality and deceit. Love is not law, and creation is tragic as well as ethical. These things confuse the obviousness of retribution. They do not, however, remove the seriousness of guilt.

Mercy is not an arbitrary forgiveness or free pardon. Pardon does not affect anything but the exterior relationship between a guilty party and the one offended; it affects the legal situation but does nothing to affect guilt or violation. Mercy bears a certain family resemblance to pardon because it is not guided by the *jus talionis*, the law of retribution. But pardon does not break out of legalism to the region of real guilt and violation. The problem mercy addresses is guilt and the weakness or wickedness that gives rise to guilt. The guilt is real, just as the wickedness is real: sin is not a guilt "feeling" or a heteronomous legal offense.

Mercy is oriented to guilt but not as pardon. Mercy cannot be understood within the context of legal metaphors. It is directed toward guilt not to forgive it but to eradicate it. Mercy shares with an ethical vision an abhorrence of cruelty but not its confidence that retribution solves the problem. Its hatred of evil is not appeased when the wicked suffer. Its hatred of evil is assuaged only when evil is itself overcome. To hurt or imprison sinners' bodies while their hearts become ever harder is no satisfaction to mercy, not because mercy is too softhearted, but because the evil remains and in fact is exaggerated in the process. Mercy disciplines its anger at wickedness and transforms it into an attack on evil itself. Mercy radicalizes ethical condemnation of evil by redeeming the evildoer and in this way destroying evil. Mercy is the desire to redeem; it is equally indifferent to clemency and to punishment. It is healing power that overcomes guilt.

Just as compassion uses whatever means are appropriate to the situation before it, mercy likewise is less interested in a particular mechanism than in securing redemption from sin. It may be that in some cases, redemption from sin is accomplished by suffering or punishment. *Crime and Punishment* represents this method of redemption. After several years in a Siberian prison, Raskolnikov was freed both from the burden of his guilt and from the interior sickness that drove him to murder. It may be that a gratuitous act of kindness done to protect or help the guilty person accomplishes redemption. The redemptive power of mercy is described in *Les Misérables* when the priest saves Jean Valjean from the police by telling them that the silver Jean had stolen from him was in reality a gift. It may be that in seeing clearly the consequences of one's acts, the vileness of them can become plain. George Bernard Shaw's *Saint Joan* describes the *metanoia* that occurs when the Chaplain, who was most vehement in desiring Joan's burning, is undone by actually seeing it.[1]

When victims of injustice find resources to defend themselves, their courage can reveal the injustice of their situation to their persecutors. The profound moral integrity of Gandhi's or Martin Luther King's nonviolent struggles condemned their opponents by the contrast between them. These movements are especially powerful expressions of the work of compassion because they simultaneously empowered victims to resist their suffering and revealed to oppressors their guilt, struggling against the evil from both directions.

Mercy, as an expression of compassion, is an interactive power. It can be extended, but it must also be accepted. It cannot be accomplished extrinsically, by fiat. It requires a response. It does not act supernaturally to make a particular punishment or clemency available to sinners. Instead, it attempts to enable them to use whatever befalls them in such a way that it will effect their redemption. Mercy empowers human beings to purge themselves of their guilt.

Judgment and condemnation of wickedness nonetheless constitute the harsh side of mercy. To be made able to see the terrible suffering and evil one is responsible for can be excruciatingly painful. Accepting responsibility and guilt is a necessary first step before guilt can be overcome. The work of judgment to purge guilt cannot be accomplished extrinsically, as if suffering an external punishment in itself purges guilt. But the internal workings of judgment through which one is able to acknowledge guilt can be infinitely more torturous. Mercy and judgment are identical in this work. It is the work of judgment both because it can be terribly painful and because it is the righteousness of God to recognize and condemn evil actions. It is the work of mercy both because it is only in this way that the sinner can be healed and purged of guilt and because mercy, as a form of compassion, is present to empower the sinner to be able to undergo judgment.

Compassion does not categorically censure all suffering or repudiate all judgment but, by mediating a sense of the contingency even of guilt, enables the suffering that arises from judgment to be redemptive. Origen interpreted the fires of hell as a metaphor for the burning pricks of conscience through which sinners first become aware of their guilt and then are purged of evil and restored to wholeness for contemplation of God. In this way he maintained a dynamic tension between the sufferings that guilt and judgment cause and the ultimately redemptive purposes of such sufferings.

It was the genius of the Hebrew prophets to see history in this light. Whatever happened to the people was interpreted as being in some way related to God's compassionate work of redemption. This sometimes led them to interpret catastrophic historical or natural disasters as expressions of divine wrath. Such an interpretation may permit suffering to be experienced as meaningful and even redemptive since for the prophets wrath was rarely more than a heartbeat away from mercy. Suffering might function to remind a people of their dependence upon God and bring them to repent of their cruelties to one another. However, a literal attribution of wrath and punishment to God deifies the "myth of punishment," and conceals the ultimately redemptive power of God.[2]

Particularly in Christianity, which has tended to see wrath and love, heaven and hell, not as sequential moments in the work of redemption, but as in eternal opposition, the metaphor of wrath has become dangerous and even blasphemous. A striking complement to the evocation of divine wrath is the depiction of God's yearning for Israel to come back, to accept the mercy God has stored for them. In the eyes of the prophets, God does not desire the death of sinners and desires even less the destruction sin causes but is helpless to turn human beings from sin and force them to accept the mercy that would heal them. It is a strange situation, as if a mother leaned as far as possible toward a child to embrace it and the child yearned for the mother but somehow they remained apart.

Sin, like suffering, erects an iron curtain between humanity and God. Unlike suffering, it is not pain itself that is the veil but hard-heartedness and guilt. Compassion labors to tear the veil of suffering. Mercy yearns to melt the hard heart of sin and free it from its cruelty. But the power of God to redeem does not force human beings to accept the compassion that is offered to them. Perhaps the ultimate mystery of human existence is our capacity to resist the eternal abyss of divine love.

The Problem of Evil

Compassion—which enables human beings to work for justice, comforts them in despair, and offers mercy to heal sin—manifests divine power. Yet human beings remain enslaved by their own guilt and cruelty and by unjust, radical suffering. Traditional theology notes this phenomenon and infers that it must be because God is punishing the human *race* for its sin (even if it appears that certain individuals suffer unjustly, they share the guilt of Adam). Divine omnipotence and justice are upheld in such a view; otherwise suffering would be intolerable—chaotic, random, meaningless. Much contemporary theology, also disturbed by this phenomenon, has opted to limit or forego divine power and replace it with divine suffering. An adequate doctrine of God must find a way of articulating divine being as both a power and a goodness. It is my hope that this analysis of love as a form of power will provide a way of doing this.

Omnipotence and Tragedy

An alternative way of construing the problem of evil appears possible. God brings forth creation out of a divine eros for life and love. Creation emerges as real alterity, as really other than God. It has its own power, its own freedom. Its created perfection lies in its autonomy, just as the perfection of divine love and power lies in God's capacity to bring about a reality that is other than Godself. Created perfection is fragile, tragically structured. The tragic structure of finitude and the human capacity for deception and cruelty together account for the possibility and actuality of suffering and evil. Because of its independence, history constitutes a "surprise center"[3] even for God. If creation is authentically other than God, it evades complete determinism at the hands of divine power. It is the risk and folly of the power of love to create that over which it has only relative control. And yet without creation, divine eros remains merely potential, inarticulate. The fragility of creation and the nonabsolute power of God culminate in the tragedy and rupture of history.

Omnipotence is the power to do whatever can be done absolutely, that is, whatever is logically possible.[4] But to overcome the tragic structure of finitude, to free animate beings from all suffering, to determine finite freedom so that it will always love the good and have the courage to pursue it—these things are not possible. The potential for suffering and evil lie in the tragic structure of finitude and cannot be overcome without destroying creation. The power to create must therefore include the power to redeem. The fragility of creation requires the continual presence of divine power to resist the evils resident in history. But it is the virtue of this power that it is not absolute, it is interactive. If this mutuality is construed as a limitation upon divine power, it is a limitation that is entailed by the alterity of finite existence and by the nature of love. It is the nature of love to desire the freedom and well-being of the beloved rather than domination. Omnipotence is not *limited* at all, but its power is to share life and mediate love. Yet because of the inexorable fragility of creation and the potential for sin, the infinite abyss of divine power and love is destined to disappointment.

Compassionate Power and History

History can resist God's power and do so with great determination and force. It does so through the evil of individuals, such as the rapist or the Klansman. It does so through an indeterminate constellation of historical, sociological, and cultural forces. An evil such as sexism is carried partly through the violence and evil of individuals. But it is possible as an institutional, historical reality because it is mediated by language, culture, economic and social policies: by a thousand almost invisible structures and powers that perpetuate prejudice and its debilitating effects. The symbol of Satan, as the power of evil that seduces individuals and communities to share his evildoing, expresses this sense that evil is irreducible to the intention of individuals. Evil seems to stand over against a community to beguile it into actions and beliefs that betray its own vision of the good. The metaphor of the ransom of the human race signifies that God's redemptive work is directed toward history itself, toward communal existence and not only toward individual souls.

The tragic structure of finitude, the fragility of freedom, the suprapersonal efficacy of history stand over against God as expressions of that which most fundamentally resists and rejects God. The problem of theodicy is history's power to reject God. History goes beyond "natural" suffering to "gross evil," evil that is absolute and irredeemable. There is no resolution to the evil of six million Jews murdered in death camps; there is no resolution to the tortured or famished bodies of black children and their parents in South Africa; there is no resolution to the tears and blood that soak the world through from crust to core. Evil must remain a surd, with no resolution, no atonement.

Beyond the power of evil to cause suffering is the power of evil to block the presence of divine compassion in its activity to redeem and comfort the world. Religion, whose role is to mediate that presence and power to the world, more characteristically obscures them. The church often incarnates and deifies misogyny and racism. Theology twists the radicality of infinite love and compassion into images of a tyrannical and cruel judge. Suffering is called divine punishment. Cruelty, callousness, legalism—all of which are expressions of the corruption of freedom—become sacred. The tools we are given to taste the beauty of the divine—scripture, the church, religion, theology, even the Messiah—cease to be windows to God and become mirrors that reflect back our own stupidity and cruelty. God is disarmed; the mediators of divine compassion speak instead for evil.

If it is possible to speak of the efficacy of divine compassion at all, it is impossible to do so in ways that would deny the existence of absolute evil: evil for which there is no atonement or vindication. Nothing in the past, present, or future will atone for the wanton, cruel destruction of human beings in death camps and torture chambers or through the structural evils of poverty, sexism, and racism. It is also impossible to speak of divine compassion or redemption without remembering that evil mars even those gifts to humanity through which redemption should be mediated. The mediators of the sacred—the church, scripture, ritual—are no less ambiguous and potentially destructive than the secular world. There is no special place of appeal or security, no institution, book, or experience that can be relied upon to protect oneself or one's community from sin and evil. If there is an actuality of redemption, it is not in some magically protected sphere that is unambiguously good or trustworthy. In speaking of divine compassion, neither the reality of radical evil nor the ambiguity and corruptions of the "means of salvation" can be forgotten.

Despite the harshness and ambiguity of history, redemption remains historical. Divine power should also be interpreted as engaged in history: directed not only toward individual hearts but toward a complex of forces that condition and are conditioned by human responsibility.

Redemption and Resistance

I argued that one of the warrants for the paradigm of love as the basis for a doctrine of God is the experience of redemption, which functions as a criterion for religious discourse. It would be a falsification of human experience to describe the human condition in such a way that this reality is denied. It would not only be a falsification, it would be a betrayal of the courage of all of those who have resisted injustice, finding the power and faith to do so in the very midst of radical evil. The clue to understanding the presence of God in history lies in the *actuality of resistance*. Resistance hints at the nonfinality of evil, attesting to the power of compassion in history.[5]

If it is acknowledged that tragedy qualifies existence, that history is ruptured by suffering, and that eschatology cannot sufficiently address these evils, redemption cannot be understood as a "New Jerusalem" in which every tear is wiped away. Redemption must be sought *in the midst* of tragedy and rupture. Redemption that occurs under the conditions of historical existence will not have the character of complete freedom from suffering, guilt, and evil; it will instead be realized as resistance to them. Redemption interpreted as resistance retains the ambiguity of life; it is not a denial or indifference to historical suffering, neither is it a despairing absorption in suffering and evil. It presupposes the perennial presence of evil but embodies an alternative to it in history, both by incarnating an opposing reality of love and justice and by laboring to limit, qualify, and heal evil wherever possible.

Following Johann B. Metz, Sharon Welch argues that one of the conditions of resistance to oppression and degradation is the "dangerous memory" of

> hope, a memory of freedom and resistance. . . . In order for there to be resistance and the affirmation that is implied in the preservation of the memory of suffering, there must be an experience that includes some degree of liberation from the devaluation of human life by the dominant apparatuses of power/knowledge. Even to resist implies a modicum of liberation and success.[6]

In the very heart of suffering and oppression, resistance to evil is possible; in this resistance divine compassion becomes incarnate. Resistance is the holy ground wherein divine presence is known and experienced.

Resistance can take many forms both within and against situations of suffering and victimization. The possibility of resisting despair and degradation in the face of a hopeless or agonizing disease witnesses to the incarnation of the power of redemption. Rebellion against tyranny, struggles for justice, and the preservation of dignity and fellowship are all examples of the power of compassion incarnate in history. In defiance of evil, a love of creation and life combines with the power to struggle against suffering. This vitality that urges history toward fulfillment and life, that enters suffering to overcome it, and that consoles and empowers human beings to resist evil might be recognized by the eyes of faith as the continuing incarnation of the power of divine love in history.

The Mediation of the Power of Compassion in History

Divine compassion may be mediated by the traditional "means of salvation": the church, the scriptures, or Torah. Certainly it is the proper function of these things to mediate the redemptive power of God to history. But it would be inappropriate to view these vehicles of redemption as unambiguous or to confine divine power to them. God is not only the Redeemer revealed in the church or scripture but also the Creator and Sustainer whose power is manifest and available throughout history and nature. The mediation of divine power must be understood as present in nature and history as well as through the apparatus of religion in order to do justice to the reality of redemption.

History preserves the "dangerous memories" of real occasions of liberation. The release of the serfs in nineteenth-century Russia, the emancipation of American slaves, the enfranchisement of American women in this century, the liberation of the Nazi death camps, the release of a prisoner of conscience, small ecological triumphs—all are moments of victory that testify to the nonfinality of the powers for domination and destruction. These are moments in history when liberation and redemption are realized and become signs of the compassionate power of God in history. They bear sacramental power as the basis of hope that the struggle for justice can, at least sometimes, be victorious. These memories can mediate power to resist suffering and evil in the present. History is the medium of life and therefore of redemption; it can manifest the compassionate power of God and function as a sacrament for human redemption, as freedom, justice, mercy, delight, and affection are realized concretely in the world.

Scripture, tradition, and the church have functioned in history to justify and deepen the oppression of women, Jews, African Americans, and people in every part of the world. Scripture itself is infected with a patriarchal bias and overtly sexist and misogynist statements. A recovery of these resources cannot overlook this history or the presence of degrading ideas internal to the tradition itself. The culpability of the Christian tradition should not come as too great a shock, though. The expectation that *any* resource, including traditional authorities, could be free of the taint of corruption expresses an unwarranted confidence in history and human "nature." A critical stance must be taken toward every resource. But beyond a hermeneutic of suspicion, a hermeneutic of recovery may be possible. For all their ambiguity, the church and scripture also can mediate the compassionate power of God in history. Scripture is rife with the preservation and sanctification of memories of the struggle against historical suffering and persecution. The story of the exodus remembers God's "mighty acts" on behalf of miserable slaves against the local world power. The prophets are passionate exponents of a vision of justice in which oppression is the final insult to God and assault on God's creation. The parables of the kingdom of God present a vision that stands in condemnation of the realities of exclusion and indifference. Paul and Jesus open a community in which the outcasts—the women and slaves—are free to claim their full humanity and participation.

> How was it possible for black people to keep their humanity together in the midst of servitude, affirming that the God of Jesus is at work in the world, liberating them from bondage? The record shows clearly that black slaves believed that just as God had delivered Moses and the Israelites from Egyptian bondage, he also will deliver black people from American slavery. . . . That truth did not come from white preachers; it came from a liberating encounter with the One who is the Author of black faith and existence.[7]

Scripture is the record of a people's experience of suffering, oppression, and hope. It can be a resource that reminds human beings of the possibility and reality of divine compassion active in history. The exodus from Egypt, Israel's release from captivity in Babylon, and the coming of the Messiah are signs or memories of God's liberating, redemptive work. They do not nullify radical suffering and evil, or provide hope that evil will be magically, unambiguously overcome, or imply that resistance to evil atones for suffering. Scripture is, in part, a legacy of God's redemptive activity in history. A *critical* appropriation of its liberating vision may serve as a way of empowering the continued struggle against oppression and suffering.

The church can be a community that mediates both a vision and a power of redemption as it comes together to discern the presence of God in its life and in the broader world. Through the sacraments and participation in a local community, people sometimes find in the church a mediator of a redeemed vision of humanity. The church can empower human beings and communities to resist the evils and suffering within and without the church. The church can also enable human beings to enjoy God and celebrate creation even when history is stained with malice and suffering. The sacrament of the eucharist contains some of these elements. It symbolizes a shared meal that enacts the fellowship of all peoples. It is a memory and a celebration of God's presence in the midst of the struggle against evil. It is an enactment and memory of redemption that can empower human beings to participate in the perennial incarnation of divine compassion.

Scripture and the church, for all of their ambiguity, still can witness to the nonfinality of evil by envisioning (and occasionally embodying) an alternative to the "principalities and powers" that dominate history. Neither history nor the church are *characterized* by their ability to resist evil. But in our tragic and broken world, any small token of the nonfinality of evil signifies the power of redemption at work against despair and evil.

History, scripture, and the church are examples of communities, memories, and events that enable human beings to envision and enact alternatives to injustice and suffering. These moments of redemption testify neither to a utopian past nor to a consummated future but rather to the possibilities of redemption within a tragically broken creation. The struggle against evil must acknowledge and honor the conditions of life, even its tragic dimension, and seek redemption within them.

A vision of historical redemption should not describe an otherworldly escape from history but a fulfillment of possibilities resident in it. Such a vision is present in the Hebrew prophets and the parables of Jesus. The symbols that emerge from the teachings by or about Jesus witness to the possibility of transformation within tragic, historical existence. Jesus' table fellowship with sinners and outcasts has a "now and not yet" character to it. It foreshadows a messianic banquet where all peoples will come together as a single family, but it also testifies to the inbreaking of such a hope into history. The sharing of food and fellowship among different classes, races, and cultures is not only an eschatological hope but a fragmentary historical accomplishment. Jesus' own act established it as a real possibility that human beings can struggle toward and even occasionally achieve. It is a "dangerous memory" of fellowship that can empower its continual, if never final or unambiguous, incarnation in history.

The parables are strange, provocative stories that turn heads and hearts toward a revision of historical existence. The gratuitous, passionate love of the Samaritan for his enemy or the father for his prodigal son represent real possibilities even within tragic existence. The strange logic of the parables is a logic for this world. In it widows and shepherds have the same concern for one lost coin or sheep as for the totality of their possessions; people are divided like sheep and goats on the basis of how well they cared for God incarnate in the hungry, the sick, and the criminal. It is a logic that orients human beings toward one another according to principles of justice, compassion, and celebration. It is a logic that stands over against the reality of despair, selfishness, sin, and cruelty, as a *real* alternative, not as an otherworldly consummation. It is a demand and a promise that it is possible to "do justice and love kindness" in concrete, historical life.

This logic and vision represent a memory and promise of historical redemption that crashes into the reality of radical evil: it is the recalcitrance of irrational, sadistic injustice and cruelty that makes this logic seem not merely utopian but eschatological. The parables of Jesus, the promises of the prophets, the modest hopes of obscure people are met with the hopelessly immense powers of evil. Evil *is* stronger than good; struggles for justice and redemption cannot hope to overcome either the tragic structures of creation or the historical realities of selfishness and violence.

Resilience and Redemption

Compassion does not overcome the power of destruction, any more than Jesus came down from the cross. The power of destruction is real; the lives, hope, sanity, and goodness that are maimed by cruelty can never be replaced or atoned for. But it is the power of divine compassion to endure, to be deathless, to be resurrected even from the ashes of despair and death. There is a resilience to divine compassion that the superior strength of evil cannot finally overcome, however real its victories. Compassion remains the ground and power of resistance, of hope, of a transformation of the future and a recovery of the past: fragments of liberation and a return to the center.

Divine compassion is the power of redemption, realized in history within its tragic structures and in the midst of rupture. Redemption, therefore, cannot mean a final victory over historical evil. It remains fragmentary, always subject to defeat. Redemption cannot mean that radical suffering and sin are not destructive, or that their destructions are irrelevant or unreal, let alone deserved. But precisely in the depth of this destruction a power remains to resist it, to thwart it, to preserve the possibility of healing. The hope of resistance and even, occasionally, the celebration of life occurs in defiance of the absoluteness of evil. Struggle and celebration are sacraments of the goodness of creation.

If the cross represents the incarnation of divine compassion in the midst of rupture, the resurrection suggests that evil is not absolute: signs of the kingdom, memories of justice and mercy break into the very midst of history. The Gospels' insistence on the physical resurrection of Jesus emphasizes the significance of his continuing presence for historical existence: redemptive power is not totally deferred to a transhistorical return in glory. The Messiah comes, is savagely executed, but remains present to the community that persists in his name. The radical presence of God in history to resist suffering, injustice, and evil does not defeat evil. But it persists, continuing to grace history with its power and beauty.

The incarnation of divine compassion occurred and occurs in the struggle against evil and in moments of celebration and delight. We can share in the work to love and liberate the earth and in doing so, we can taste the tender and passionate love of

God for the world. On the edge of doom, we are obliged not only to resist evil but to celebrate with God the loveliness of life. Delight in creation need not be a betrayal of the struggle against evil or an indifference to those who are destroyed by pain or guilt. It is defiance of the dominion of evil, a sacrament to the unity of the divine eros and divine compassion, without which compassion and resistance veer too near despair.

Faith might be understood as an ever-deepening sense of the long sorrow of the world together with a vision and enactment of the compassion of God for creation, a light always deeper than the darkness of evil. The two can never be separated, love for life can never be isolated from work to alleviate its suffering: desire and compassion are equally essential elements of love.

Theodicy cannot explain away evil or make evil into any good. It can only hope to illuminate the radical love of God that is not overcome by evil, that is poured out inexhaustibly over all creation. In seeing and tasting this love, human beings are not only made wise like Job; they themselves come to burn with incandescent compassion for the world, to feel the grief of the world without being destroyed by it, without being paralyzed against resistance by despair. Instead they are empowered for the work of resistance. In the midst of evil is the fire that emerges out of the abyss of divinity, the flame that is never quenched. The infinite tenderness of love and the ferocity of divinity burn together through the ages of life's long struggle for redemption.

> Though the fig tree do not blossom,
>   nor fruit be on the vines,
> the produce of the olive fail
>   and the fields yield no food,
> the flock be cut off from the fold
>   and there be no herd in the stalls,
> yet I will rejoice in the LORD,
>   I will joy in the God of my salvation.
> GOD, the Lord, is my strength;
>   he makes my feet like hinds' feet,
>   he makes me tread upon my high places.
>   Habakkuk 3:17–19

Notes

Full publishing information not given here appears in the Selected Bibliography.

Chapter 1: Tragic Vision

1. Fyodor Dostoevsky, *The Brothers Karamazov,* tr. Andrew H. Mac-Andrew, 293.

2. From "Women and Torture," *File on Torture* (Amnesty International), July 1985, 1.

3. Immanuel Kant, *An Inquiry Critical and Metaphysical, Into the Grounds of Proof for the Existence of God and Into Theodicy,* tr. John Richardson (London, 1819); cited in Harold M. Schulweis, *Evil and the Morality of God,* 120.

4. Thomas Aquinas, *Summa Theologica* 1.22.2 reply 2.

5. Miguel de Unamuno, *The Tragic Sense of Life,* tr. J. E. Crawford Flitch.

6. Max Scheler, "On the Tragic"; Karl Jaspers, *Tragedy Is Not Enough,* tr. Harold A. T. Reiche, Harry T. Moore, Karl W. Deutsch; Nicolas Berdyaev, *The Destiny of Man* and *The Meaning of History,* tr. George Reavey.

7. W. Lee Humphreys, *The Tragic Vision and the Hebrew Tradition,* 3.

8. Humphreys, *The Tragic Vision,* 6.

9. Scheler, "On the Tragic," 182.

10. Aeschylus, *Prometheus Bound,* 158–162.

11. Another interpretation of Antigone's dilemma would emphasize the tragic consequences that arise from an excessive zeal for one value that cannot acknowledge any other value. Even morality can become self-destructive or wanton when it is blind to other values. See Martha Nussbaum, *The Fragility of Goodness: Luck and Ethics in Greek Tragedy and Philosophy.*

12. Aeschylus, *Prometheus Bound,* 1090–1093.

13. Jaspers, *Tragedy Is Not Enough,* 102.

14. Humphreys, *The Tragic Vision,* 140.

15. Dostoevsky, *The Brothers Karamazov,* 290–291.

16. Emil L. Fackenheim, *To Mend the World: Foundations of Future Jewish Thought,* 192–193.

17. Rebecca S. Chopp, *The Praxis of Suffering,* 2, 3.

18. See, for example, Thomas Aquinas, *Summa Theologica,* Q. 47.

19. Berdyaev, *The Destiny of Man,* 154.

20. John B. Cobb, Jr., and David Ray Griffin, *Process Theology: An Introductory Exposition,* 71.

21. Jean Nabert, *Elements for an Ethic,* tr. William J. Petrek, 26.

Chapter 2: The Rupture of Creation

1. Primo Levi, *Survival in Auschwitz,* tr. Stuart Wolf (New York: Orion Press, 1959), 82; quoted in Emil L. Fackenheim, *To Mend the World,* 25.

2. Gustavo Gutiérrez, *A Theology of Liberation: History, Politics, and Salvation,* tr. and ed. Sister Caridad Inda and John Eagleson, 195.

3. Hannah Arendt, *Eichmann in Jerusalem: A Report on the Banality of Evil,* 86.

4. Isak Dinesen, *Out of Africa* and *Shadows on the Grass,* 291.

5. Arendt, *Eichmann in Jerusalem,* 106.

6. Fackenheim, *To Mend the World,* 12.

7. Allan Boesak, "Liberation Theology in South Africa," 170.

8. Dorothee Soelle, *Suffering,* tr. Everett R. Kalin, 32.

9. Rebecca S. Chopp, *The Praxis of Suffering,* 2.

10. Flora Rheta Schreiber, *Sybil* (Chicago: Henry Regnery Co., 1973).

11. D. H. Lawrence, *Lady Chatterley's Lover.*

12. Fackenheim, *To Mend the World,* 209.

13. Quoted in ibid., 217.

14. Emmanuel Levinas, *Collected Philosophical Papers,* tr. Alphonso Lingis, 16.

15. Alice Walker, *The Color Purple,* 149.

16. E. S. Gerstenberger and W. Schrage, *Suffering,* tr. John E. Steely, 13.

17. Quoted in Fackenheim, *To Mend the World,* 25.

18. Gabriel Marcel, *Homo Viator: Introduction to a Metaphysics of Hope,* tr. Emma Craufurd, 41.

19. Fackenheim, *To Mend the World,* 224–225.

20. Simone Weil, *Waiting for God,* tr. Emma Craufurd, 122–123.

21. Fackenheim, *To Mend the World,* 216.

22. J. R. R. Tolkien, *The Return of the King,* 215.

23. Weil, *Waiting for God,* 119–120.

24. Alex Haley, *Roots: The Saga of an American Family,* 205–206.

25. See chapter 1.

26. Emmanuel Levinas, *Existence and Existents,* tr. Alphonso Lingis, 91.

27. Ibid.

28. Fyodor Dostoevsky, *The Brothers Karamazov,* 295.

Chapter 3: A Phenomenology of Compassion

1. "The growth of personal ideas through intercourse . . . implies a growing power of sympathy, of entering into and sharing the minds of other persons. To converse with another through words, looks, or other symbols means to have more or less understanding or communion with him." Charles Horton Cooley, *Human Nature and the Social Order,* 136.

2. Edith Stein, *On the Problem of Empathy,* tr. Waltraut Stein, 10–11. Scheler is equally insistent on this point: "*All* fellow-feeling involves *intentional reference* of the feeling of joy or sorrow to the other person's experience. . . . That is, *my* commiseration and *his* suffering are phenomenologically *two different facts.*" Max Scheler, *The Nature of Sympathy,* tr. Peter Heath, 13.

3. Scheler, *The Nature of Sympathy,* 39.

4. Stein, *On the Problem of Empathy,* 13–14.

5. Scheler, *The Nature of Sympathy,* 18.

6. Ibid., 58.

7. The region that is being described as an "enduring disposition" has been set forth through a variety of metaphors and analyses. See Jonathan Edwards's analysis of affections, particularly "holy love," in *Treatise Concerning the Religious Affections:* Holy love is neither understanding, nor action, nor habit, nor principle, but an enduring disposition that integrates the whole of human being including consciousness and action. Cf. Marcel's analysis of "availability" as a disposition of openness to being, "welcoming" whatever confronts one, in Gabriel Marcel, *The Mystery of Being,* tr. G. S. Fraser, vol. 1, ch. 6; or Joe McCown, *Availability: Gabriel Marcel and the Phenomenology of Human Openness.* Schleiermacher's analysis of "feeling" or immediate self-consciousness in Sections 3 and 4 of *The Christian Faith,* ed. H. R. Mackintosh and J. S. Stewart, is a particularly thorough phenomenology of what I am calling an enduring disposition. All of these analyses try to describe an aspect of consciousness that underlies, integrates, and gives a determinate quality to the specific moments and elements of self-consciousness.

8. Anders Nygren, *Agape and Eros,* tr. Philip S. Watson. Gene Outka contrasts rejoicing love with Reinhold Niebuhr's insistence that love be self-sacrificing and free from any glimmerings of self-interest. Gene Outka, *Agape: An Ethical Analysis,* 34–35.

9. This is a quotation from one of the mothers of the Plaza de Mayo in Argentina, taken from an Amnesty International brochure, "Women's Human Rights Denied."

10. This is how M. C. D'Arcy describes (and criticizes) Thomas Aquinas's depiction of love as a disinterested wishing another well: "This seems a poor substitute for the glory of Agape, and even to human lovers, the heats of love must seem poorly described by such a cool and refrigerating name as benevolence." M. C. D'Arcy, *The Mind and Heart of Love,* 69.

11. Cooley, *Human Nature,* 137.

12. David Ernest Cartwright, *"The Ethical Significance of Sympathy, Compassion, and Pity,"* 324.

13. The capacity to recognize the humanity and dignity of a sufferer is perhaps the most miraculous of compassion's gifts. As Simone Weil notes in her essay "The Love of God and Affliction": "Men have the same carnal nature as animals. If a hen is hurt, the others rush upon it, attacking it with their beaks. This phenomenon is as automatic as gravitation. Our senses attach all the scorn, all the revulsion, all the hatred that our reason attaches to crime, to affliction. Except for those whose whole soul is inhabited by Christ, everybody despises the afflicted to some extent, although practically no one is conscious of it." "When [compassion for the afflicted] is really found we have a more astounding miracle than walking on water, healing the sick, or even raising the dead." *Waiting for God,* 122, 120.

14. Victor Hugo, *Les Misérables,* tr. Charles E. Wilbour, 26–27.

15. Richard E. Creel uses the example of a parent who must inflict a painful, unpleasant medical treatment on a child. He argues that because the parent knows that the medicine is for the child's good and in fact is a condition for healing, the parent will feel no sorrow, hence no compassion. *Divine Impassibility: An Essay in Philosophical Theology,* 122. I would think, though, that such calculating indifference to pain is inadequate as a description of parental love in the face of a child's suffering.

16. Fyodor Dostoevsky, *Crime and Punishment,* tr. Constance Garnett, 354.

17. *New Schaff-Herzog Encyclopedia of Religious Knowledge,* art. "Justice" (Grand Rapids: Baker Book House, 1949–50).

18. Abraham Heschel, *The Prophets,* 1:201.

19. Ibid., 1:204, citing E. N. Cahn, *The Sense of Injustice* (New York: New York University Press, 1949), 13.

20. See note 17.

21. Paul Tillich, *Love, Power, and Justice,* 84, 88.

22. Heschel, *The Prophets,* 1:216.

23. Ibid., 2:65. The outrage of the mothers of the Plaza de Mayo when Argentina's government granted immunity from prosecution for human rights violations to all but the most senior officers is an example of both the danger and injustice of indiscriminate clemency. "Amnesty International believes that any law granting immunity from prosecution to individuals charged with criminal responsibility for grave violations of human rights runs the risk of being seen as encouraging or facilitating future abuses." *Amnesty International Newsletter* 16/12 (December 1987): 4.

24. James A. Mohler, *Dimensions of Love: East and West,* 33.

25. "Urgent Action Update," *Amnesty International Newsletter,* May 1987.

26. Jean Baker Miller, *Toward a New Psychology of Women,* 115–116.

27. Gustavo Gutiérrez, *A Theology of Liberation,* tr. Sister Caridad Inda and John Eagleson, 26.

28. E. A. Burtt, ed., *The Teachings of the Compassionate Buddha: Early Discourses, The Dhammapada, and Later Basic Writings,* 44–46.

29. J. R. R. Tolkien, *The Fellowship of the Ring,* 69.

30. Ibid., 282.

31. Ibid., 282–283.

32. Simone Weil, *The Simone Weil Reader,* ed. George A. Panichas, 358.

33. David Ray Griffin, "The Omnipotence Fallacy," *God, Power, and Evil: A Process Theodicy.*

Chapter 4: A Phenomenology of Divine Love

1. Thomas Aquinas, *Summa Theologica* 1.21.3.

2. Emmanuel Levinas, *Totality and Infinity: An Essay in Exteriority,* tr. Alphonso Lingis, 63.

3. Pseudo-Dionysius the Areopagite, *The Divine Names and Mystical Theology,* tr. John D. Jones, *The Divine Names* 588.B.

4. Friedrich Schleiermacher, *The Christian Faith,* 732.

5. Thomas Aquinas, *Summa Theologica* 1.3.

6. Jacob Boehme, *Mysterium Magnum: Or an Exposition of the First Book of Moses Called Genesis,* 1.1.

7. Paul Tillich, *Systematic Theology,* 1:250–251.

8. Ibid., 1:251.

9. Thomas Aquinas, *Summa Theologica* 1.44.4; 5.4.

10. Emmanuel Levinas, *Collected Philosophical Papers,* 57.

11. A metaphysical version of this phenomenology of love that emphasizes creativity and relationship, movement and dialectics, can be found most recently in process philosophy. Plotinus, Jacob Boehme, Hegel, Tillich, and Berdyaev also offer philosophical expressions of this more dialectical and relational conceptual paradigm.

12. Boehme, *Mysterium Magnum* 3.5.

13. Tillich, *Systematic Theology,* 1:252.

14. Norman C. Habel, *The Book of Job,* 533.

15. Ibid., 579.

16. "Love neither rules, nor is it unmoved; also it is a little oblivious as to morals." Alfred North Whitehead, *Process and Reality,* corrected edition, ed. David Ray Griffin and Donald W. Sherburne, 343.

17. Gerard Manley Hopkins, "As Kingfishers Catch Fire," *Poems of Gerard Manley Hopkins,* 53.

Chapter 5: Divine Compassion and the Problem of Evil

1. "I let them do it. If I had known I would have torn her from their hands. . . . It is so easy to talk when you don't know. You madden yourself with words: you damn yourself because it feels grand to throw oil on the flaming

hell of your own temper. But when it is brought home to you; when you see the thing you have done; when it is blinding your eyes, stifling your nostrils, tearing your heart, then—then . . . I am in hell for evermore." George Bernard Shaw, *Saint Joan,* scene vi.

2. "The threat of punishment is one of the most prominent themes of prophetic orations. Yet the prophets themselves seem to have questioned the efficacy of punishment." Abraham Heschel, *The Prophets,* 1:187. He continues, "The prophets . . . discovered that suffering does not necessarily bring about purification, nor is punishment effective as a deterrent. The futility of chastisement was a problem that occupied the minds of the prophets" (1:188).

3. Buber, *Sehertum. Anfang und Ausgang,* 59.

4. Thomas Aquinas, *Summa Theologica* 1.25.3.

5. The discovery of various forms of resistance to the Holocaust within the death camps themselves provides Fackenheim with his clue to the possibility of a "mending of the world."

"Now our ecstatic thought must point to *their* . . . resistance in life—as *ontologically ultimate. Resistance in that extremity was a way of being. For our thought now, it is an ontological category.*" Emil L. Fackenheim, *To Mend the World,* 248.

6. Sharon Welch, *Communities of Resistance and Solidarity,* 39.

7. James H. Cone, *God of the Oppressed,* 11.

Selected Bibliography

Aeschylus. *Prometheus Bound.* In *Chief Patterns of World Drama: Aeschylus to Anderson.* 2d ed. Edited by William Smith Clark. New York: Houghton Mifflin Co., 1946.

Amnesty International. *Amnesty International Newsletter,* December 1987.

———. *File on Torture,* July 1985.

———. "Women's Human Rights Denied." Brochure, Amnesty International, 1983.

———. "Urgent Action Update." *Amnesty International Newsletter,* May 1987.

Arendt, Hannah. *Eichmann in Jerusalem: A Report on the Banality of Evil.* New York: Penguin Books, 1963; rev. and enlarged, 1965).

Aristotle. *Poetics.* In *The Rhetoric and Poetics of Aristotle.* Translated by W. Rhys Roberts and Ingram Bywater. New York: Random House, Modern Library, 1954.

Augustine. *City of God.* Translated by Henry Bettenson. Introduction by David Knowles. New York and London: Penguin Books, 1972.

Barth, Karl. *Church Dogmatics* 4/2. Edited by G. W. Bromiley and T. F. Torrance, translated by G. W. Bromiley. Edinburgh: T. & T. Clark, 1958.

Bauckham, Richard. " 'Only the Suffering God Can Help': Divine Passibility in Modern Theology," *Themelios* 9, no. 3 (1984).

Berdyaev, Nicolas. *The Destiny of Man.* New York: Harper & Row, Harper Torchbooks, 1960.

———. *The Meaning of History.* Translated by George Reavey. London: Geofrey Bles, Centenary Press, 1936.

Berndtson, Arthur. *Power, Form and Mind.* East Brunswick, N.J.: Associated University Presses, 1981.

Boehme, Jacob. *Mysterium Magnum: Or an Exposition of the First Book of Moses Called Genesis.* Translated by John Sparrow. London: John M. Watkins, 1924.

———. "Six Theosophical Questions," in *On the Election of Grace and*

Questions Theosophical. Translated by John Rolleston Earle. London: Constable & Co., 1930.

Boesak, Allan. "Liberation Theology in South Africa," in *African Theology en Route.* Edited by Kofi Appiah-Kubi and Sergio Torres. Maryknoll, N.Y.: Orbis Books, 1981.

Brown, Robert F. *The Later Philosophy of Schilling: The Influence of Boehme on the Works of 1809–1815.* Cranbury, N.J.: Associated University Presses, 1977.

Buber, Martin. *Between Man and Man.* Translated by Ronald Gregor Smith. London: Routledge & Kegan Paul, 1947.

_____. *I and Thou.* 2d ed. Translated by Ronald Gregor Smith. New York: Charles Scribner's Sons, 1958.

_____. *Images of Good and Evil.* Translated by Michael Bullock. London: Routledge & Kegan Paul, 1952.

_____. *The Origin and Meaning of Hasidism.* Edited and translated by Maurice Friedman. New York: Horizon Press, 1960.

_____. *Sehertum. Anfang und Ausgang.* Cologne: Jakob Hegner, 1955.

Burtt, E. A., editor. *The Teachings of the Compassionate Buddha: Early Discourses, The Dhammapada, and Later Basic Writings.* New York: New American Library, Mentor Books, 1955.

Calvin, John. *The Institutes.* 2 vols. Library of Christian Classics. Translated by Ford Lewis Battles. Edited by John T. McNeill. Philadelphia: Westminster Press, 1960.

Cartwright, David Ernest. "The Ethical Significance of Sympathy, Compassion, and Pity." Ph.D. dissertation, University of Wisconsin–Madison, 1981.

Chopp, Rebecca S. *The Praxis of Suffering.* Maryknoll, N.Y.: Orbis Books, 1986.

Cobb, John B., Jr., and David Ray Griffin. *Process Theology: An Introductory Exposition.* Philadelphia: Westminster Press, 1976.

Cone, James H. *God of the Oppressed.* New York: Seabury Press, 1975.

Cooley, Charles Horton. *Human Nature and the Social Order.* New York: Charles Scribner's Sons, 1902. Reprint, New Brunswick, N.J.: Transaction Books, 1983.

Creel, Richard E. *Divine Impassibility: An Essay in Philosophical Theology.* Cambridge: Cambridge University Press, 1986.

D'Arcy, M. C. *The Mind and Heart of Love.* New York: Henry Holt & Co., 1947.

Dinesen, Isak. *Out of Africa* and *Shadows on the Grass.* New York: Random House, 1937. Reprint, New York: Vintage Books, 1985.

Dostoevsky, Fyodor. *The Brothers Karamazov.* Translated by Andrew H. MacAndrew. New York: Bantam Books, 1970, 1981.

_____. *Crime and Punishment.* Translated by Constance Garnett. New York: Bantam Books, 1959.

Edwards, Jonathan. *Select Works of Jonathan Edwards.* Vol. 3. *Treatise Concerning the Religious Affections.* London: Banner of Truth Trust, 1961.

Fackenheim, Emil L. *To Mend the World: Foundations of Future Jewish Thought.* New York: Schocken Books, 1982.

Farley, Edward. "Comment on David Tracy: 'Hermeneutics as Discourse Analysis: Sociality, History, and Religion,' " in *Intersoggettività Socialità Religione (Archivio di Filosofia* 54/1–3 [1986]).

Gerstenberger, E. S., and W. Schrage. *Suffering.* Translated by John E. Steely. Nashville: Abingdon Press, 1980.

Greene, William Chase. *Moira: Fate, Good, and Evil in Greek Thought.* Cambridge, Mass.: Harvard University Press, 1944.

Griffin, David Ray. *God, Power, and Evil: A Process Theodicy.* Philadelphia: Westminster Press, 1976.

Gutiérrez, Gustavo. *A Theology of Liberation: History, Politics, and Salvation.* Translated by Sister Caridad Inda and John Eagleson. Maryknoll, N.Y.: Orbis Books, 1973.

Habel, Norman C. *The Book of Job.* Old Testament Library. Philadelphia: Westminster Press, 1985.

Haley, Alex. *Roots: The Saga of an American Family.* Garden City, N.Y.: Doubleday & Co., 1976.

Hall, Douglas John. *God and Human Suffering.* Minneapolis: Augsburg Publishing House, 1986.

Heidegger, Martin. *Being and Time.* Translated by John Macquarrie and Edward Robinson. New York: Harper & Row, 1962.

Heschel, Abraham. *The Prophets.* 2 vols. New York: Harper & Row, 1962. Reprint, New York: Harper Torchbooks, 1969–72.

Hodgson, P. C. *Jesus: Word and Presence.* Philadelphia: Fortress Press, 1971.

Hopkins, Gerard Manley. *Poems of Gerard Manley Hopkins.* 2d ed. Edited by Robert Bridges. London: Oxford University Press, 1930.

Hugo, Victor. *Les Misérables.* Translated by Charles E. Wilbour. Abridged and introduced by James K. Robinson. New York: Ballantine Books, Fawcett Premier Book, 1961.

Humphreys, W. Lee. *The Tragic Vision and the Hebrew Tradition.* Philadelphia: Fortress Press, 1985.

Jaspers, Karl. *Tragedy Is Not Enough.* Translated by Harald A. T. Reiche, Harry T. Moore, Karl W. Deutsch. Boston: Beacon Press, 1952. Reprint, Hamden, Conn.: Shoe String Press, Archon Books, 1969.

Julian of Norwich. *Showings.* Translated by Edmund Colledge and James Walsh. Classics of Western Spirituality. New York: Paulist Press, 1978.

Kant, Immanuel. *Metaphysical Elements of Justice: Part One of the Metaphysics of Morals.* Translated with introduction by John Ladd. Indianapolis: Bobbs-Merrill Co., 1965.

Kaufman, Walter. *Tragedy and Philosophy.* Garden City, N.Y.: Doubleday & Co., 1968.

Kierkegaard, Søren. *The Concept of Anxiety: A Simple Psychologically Orienting Deliberation on the Dogmatic Issue of Hereditary Sin.* Edited and translated by Reidar Thomte. Princeton, N.J.: Princeton University Press, 1980.

———. *The Sickness Unto Death* in *Fear and Trembling and The Sickness Unto Death.* Translated with an introduction by Walter Lowrie. Princeton, N.J.: Princeton University Press, 1941.

———. *Training in Christianity.* Translated and introduced by Walter Lowrie. Princeton, N.J.: Princeton University Press, 1967.

Lawrence, D. H. *Lady Chatterley's Lover.* With an afterword by Harry T. Moore. New York: Signet Books, 1959.

Levinas, Emmanuel. *Collected Philosophical Papers.* Translated by Alphonso Lingis. Dordrecht: Martinus Nijhoff, 1987.

———. *Ethics and Infinity: Conversations with Philippe Nemo.* Translated by Richard A. Cohen. Pittsburgh: Duquesne University Press, 1985.

———. *Existence and Existents.* Translated by Alphonso Lingis. The Hague: Martinus Nijhoff, 1978.

———. *Totality and Infinity: An Essay in Exteriority.* Translated by Alphonso Lingis. Pittsburgh: Duquesne University Press, 1969.

McCown, Joe. *Availability: Gabriel Marcel and the Phenomenology of Human Openness.* Missoula, Mont.: Scholars Press, 1978.

McFague, Sallie. *Models of God: Theology for an Ecological, Nuclear Age.* Philadelphia: Fortress Press, 1987.

McGill, Arthur C. *Suffering: A Test of Theological Method.* Philadelphia: Westminster Press, 1982.

Maimonides, Moses. *The Guide for the Perplexed.* 2d ed. Translated by M. Friedlander. New York: Dover Publications, 1956.

Marcel, Gabriel. *Creative Fidelity.* Translated by Robert Rosthal. New York: Farrar, Straus, 1964.

———. *The Existential Background of Human Dignity.* Cambridge, Mass.: Harvard University Press, 1963.

———. *Homo Viator: Introduction to a Metaphysics of Hope.* Translated by Emma Craufurd. London: Victor Gollancz, 1951. Reprint, New York: Harper & Brothers, 1962.

———. *The Mystery of Being.* Vol 1. Translated by G. S. Fraser. London: Harvill Press, 1950.

Maxwell, Natalie. *Great Compassion: The Chief Cause of Bodhisattvas.* Ann Arbor, Mich.: University Microfilms International, 1979.

Miller, Jean Baker. *Toward a New Psychology of Women.* Boston: Beacon Press, 1976.

Mitchell, Stephen, translator; with introduction. *The Book of Job.* Berkeley, Calif.: North Point Press, 1987.

Moberly, Elizabeth. *Suffering, Innocent and Guilty.* London: SPCK, 1978.

Mohler, James A. *Dimensions of Love: East and West.* Garden City, N.Y.: Doubleday & Co., 1975.

Nabert, Jean. *Elements for an Ethic.* Translated by William J. Petrek. Evanston, Ill.: Northwestern University Press, 1969.

Niebuhr, H. Richard, et al. *The Purpose of the Church and Its Ministry.* New York: Harper & Row, 1956.

Nussbaum, Martha. *The Fragility of Goodness: Luck and Ethics in Greek Tragedy and Philosophy.* Cambridge: Cambridge University Press, 1986.

Nygren, Anders. *Agape and Eros.* Translated by Philip S. Watson. London: SPCK, 1953.

Outka, Gene. *Agape: An Ethical Analysis.* New Haven, Conn.: Yale University Press, 1972.

Owen, Thomas. *Phenomenology and Intersubjectivity: Contemporary Interpretations of the Interpersonal Situation.* The Hague: Martinus Nijhoff, 1970.

Plato. *The Symposium* in *Plato: The Collected Dialogues Including the Letters.* Edited by Edith Hamilton and Huntington Cairns. Princeton, N.J.: Princeton University Press, 1961.

Plotinus. *The Enneads.* Translated by Stephen Mackenna and B. S. Page. Chicago: Encyclopaedia Britannica, 1952.

Pseudo-Dionysius the Areopagite. *The Divine Names and Mystical Theology.* Translation and introduction by John D. Jones. Milwaukee: Marquette University Press, 1980.

Rahner, Karl. *Foundations of the Christian Faith: An Introduction to the Idea of Christianity.* Translated by William V. Dych. New York: Crossroad Publishing Co., 1984.

Ricoeur, Paul. *The Conflict of Interpretations: Essays in Hermeneutics.* Edited by Don Ihde. Evanston, Ill.: Northwestern University Press, 1974.

_____ . *Fallible Man: Philosophy of the Will.* Translated by Charles Kelbley. Chicago: Henry Regnery Co., 1965.

_____ . *Freud and Philosophy: An Essay on Interpretation.* Translated by Denis Savage. New Haven, Conn.: Yale University Press, 1970.

_____ . *The Symbolism of Evil.* Boston: Beacon Press, 1967.

Ruether, Rosemary Radford. *Sexism and God-talk: Toward a Feminist Theology.* Boston: Beacon Press, 1983.

Sartre, Jean-Paul. *The Philosophy of Jean-Paul Sartre.* Edited and introduced by Robert Denoon Cumming. New York: Random House, Vintage Books, 1965.

Schechter, Solomon. *Some Aspects of Rabbinic Theology.* New York: Macmillan Co., 1910.

Scheler, Max. *The Nature of Sympathy.* Translated by Peter Heath. Hamden, Conn.: Shoe String Press, Archon Books, 1954.

_____ . "On the Tragic," *Crosscurrents* 4, no. 2 (Winter 1954), 178–191.

Schilling, Paul. *God and Human Anguish.* Nashville: Abingdon Press, 1977.

Schreiber, Flora Rheta. *Sybil.* Chicago: Henry Regnery Co., 1973.

Schulweis, Harold. *Evil and the Morality of God.* Cincinnati: Hebrew Union College Press, 1984.

Schutz, Alfred. *The Phenomenology of the Social World.* Evanston, Ill.: Northwestern University Press, 1967.

Schleiermacher, Friedrich. *The Christian Faith.* Edited by H. R. Mackintosh and J. S. Stewart. New York: Charles Scribner's Sons, 1928; reprint, Philadelphia: Fortress Press, 1977.

Scott, Nathan, Jr., editor. *Tragic Vision and the Christian Faith.* New York: Association Press, 1957.

Sewall, Richard B. *Tragic Vision.* 2d ed. New Haven, Conn.: Yale University Press, 1980.

Shaw, George Bernard. *Saint Joan: A Chronicle Play in Six Scenes and an Epilogue.* Leipzig: Bernard Tauchnitz, n.d.

Soelle, Dorothee. *Suffering.* Translated by Everett R. Kalin. Philadelphia: Fortress Press, 1975.

Song, C. S. *The Compassionate God.* Maryknoll, N.Y.: Orbis Books, 1982.

Stein, Edith. *On the Problem of Empathy.* Translated by Waltraut Stein. The Hague: Martinus Nijhoff, 1964.

Stuermann, Walter E. *The Divine Destroyer.* Philadelphia: Westminster Press, 1967.

Thelakat, Paul. "Process and Privation: Aquinas and Whitehead on Evil," *International Philosophical Quarterly* 26, no. 3 (September 1986).

Theunissen, Michael. *The Other: Studies in the Social Ontology of Husserl, Heidegger, Sartre, and Buber.* Cambridge, Mass.: MIT Press, 1984.

Thomas Aquinas. *Providence and Predestination* from *Truth, Questions 5 and 6.* Translation and introduction by Robert W. Mulligan. South Bend, Ind.: Regnery/Gateway, 1961.

———. *Summa Theologica* in *Basic Writings of Saint Thomas Aquinas.* 2 vols. Edited and translated by Anton C. Pegis. New York: Random House, 1945.

Tillich, Paul. *Love, Power, and Justice: Ontological Analyses and Ethical Applications.* New York: Oxford University Press, 1960.

———. *Systematic Theology.* 3 vols. Chicago: University of Chicago Press, 1951–63.

———. *Theology of Culture.* Edited by Robert C. Kimball. New York: Oxford University Press, 1959.

Tolkien, J. R. R. *The Lord of the Rings.* Vol. 1, *The Fellowship of the Ring;* vol. 2, *The Two Towers;* vol. 3, *The Return of the King.* Rev. ed. London: George Allen & Unwin, 1966.

Unamuno, Miguel de. *The Tragic Sense of Life.* Translated by J. E. Crawford Flitch. 1913. New York: Dover Publications, 1954.

Walker, Alice. *The Color Purple.* New York: Harcourt Brace Jovanovich, 1982.

Weil, Simone. *Waiting for God.* Translated by Emma Craufurd. New York: G. P. Putnam's Sons, 1951. Reprint, New York: Harper & Row, Harper Colophon Books, 1973.

_____. *The Simone Weil Reader.* Edited by George A. Panichas. New York: David McKay Co., 1977.

Welch, Sharon. *Communities of Resistance and Solidarity: A Feminist Theology of Liberation.* Maryknoll, N.Y.: Orbis Books, 1985.

Whitehead, Alfred North. *Adventures of Ideas.* New York: Macmillan Co., 1933.

_____. *Process and Reality.* Corrected edition. Edited by David Ray Griffin and Donald W. Sherburne. New York: Macmillan Publishing Co., 1978.

Index of Names